FINLEY CARPENTER

THE SKINNER PRIMER

Behind Freedom and Dignity

Foreword by Jerome Kagan

THE FREE PRESS
A Division of Macmillan Publishing Co., Inc.
NEW YORK

Collier Macmillan Publishers
LONDON

The Free Press
A Division of Macmillan Publishing Co., Inc.
866 Third Avenue, New York, N.Y. 10022

Collier–Macmillan Canada Ltd.

Library of Congress Catalog Card Number: 73–16603

Printed in the United States of America

printing number
2   3   4   5   6   7   8   9   10

Library of Congress Cataloging in Publication Data

Carpenter, Finley.
    The Skinner primer.

    1. Operant behavior. 2. Free will and determinism.
3. Skinner, Burrhus Frederic, 1904-   I. Title.
BF319.5.06C28   1974   150'.19'434   73-16603
ISBN 0-02-905290-4

Contents

Foreword

"What is man?" has always been a question of priority for philosophers and psychologists. No matter how many different answers are offered, we react to each new reply with feeling—threatened by some descriptions, flattered by others, but always bored by statements that avoid declaring whether man is good or bad. As with most profound themes, the simplicity of the question effectively disguises its controversy and complexity. To the naturalist, man is an animal trying to adapt to varied social and physical contexts; to the economist, he is consumer, investor, and creator of capital; to the philosopher, he is a generator of propositions who continually confuses the relations among experience, inference, and the language he chooses to describe both of those processes. To B. F. Skinner, he is a reservoir of possible actions whose actualized profile is finely controlled by the history of different outcomes that followed close upon each of those actions. The single, powerful assumption that the effects of our prior actions are the hands that sculpt our current behavioral posture, carried to its limit, leads Skinner to question the autonomous control each of us has over our own behavior and to issue a challenge to those who think man has some measure of freedom.

A major function of science is to show, to everyone's amazement, that powerful subjective truths are occasionally false. Medieval man was convinced of the validity of the phenomenological truth that the earth stood still while the sun moved. It is the highest tribute to the enterprise of science and to man's respect for rationality that he was willing to replace that attitude with Copernicus' more rational one. Might this be true for freedom? Most of us are convinced that most of the time we are in firm control of whether we will say yes or no to a clerk, choose meat or fish at a restaurant, spank our children or chastise them. Indeed, the consciousness of being unsure of the relative efficacy of too many alternative choices is a common source of psychic distress. Yet here comes Skinner, a little like Copernicus, telling us that our phenomenology is defective and we are deluded if we believe that we control our actions. They are, on the contrary, under the firm stewardship of the past, continually monitored by the invisible happenings of yesterday, by changes that occurred deep within our nervous system on the many times we displayed a particular action in the situation we are in at the moment. Such a challenge to our sense of freedom and dignity has irritated and energized many and given solace to only a few.

Unfortunately, the reactions to *Beyond Freedom and Dignity* were less the product of a dispassionate analysis of Skinner's ideas than a defensive reaction to the anxiety his theme created. Finley Carpenter has done us a high service by explicating, in plain and accurate language, Skinner's thesis, giving as much space to its strengths as to its weaknesses and suggesting that Skinner's neglect of alternative meanings of freedom renders his position less potent than both his antagonists and his supporters believe.

Carpenter's thesis is that Skinner has limited his concept of freedom to the notions of escape from, and avoidance of, distress and has ignored man's reflections on the matter. Carpenter has detected and carefully described the two faults in the Skinnerian structure: the commitment to an external determinism, and a reluctance to acknowledge the central role of human thought. He wisely notes that the question of determinism is ultimately indeterminate—a question that belongs to metaphysics, not to science. Carpenter's analysis of determinism in behavior resembles Bohr's famous "complementarity" hypothesis posed to solve problems in atomic physics raised by quantum mechanics.

Carpenter suggests that, depending on the problem, we alternate between the mental postures of freedom and determinism. He argues that man *must* believe he has *some* measure of control, implying that if nature were prone to award her offspring adaptive traits she would have given man a sense of control. Without that prize, man is psychically and behaviorally impotent; with no accommodation to the real impositions placed upon him, man would destroy himself fighting forces for which he is no match.

Carpenter realizes that the mind is not yoked slavishly to reality, and that some of its covert inventions are as real as its overt actions. If man *believes* he is free, he *is* free—although that sentence is untrue if the adjective is a color or a weight. With skill and good sense, Carpenter applies his analysis of freedom to central issues in education and society. His analysis of the promises and problems of a Walden II for America places man's irrepressible creativity in the position of therapist calming the nervous apprehensions of those who fear "big brother."

This wise book is written with grace, reason, minimal prejudice, and a profound understanding of the sensitivities that surround the serious challenge contained in Skinner's thesis. Readers will enjoy it on their first study and I suspect will, as I have, return to its pages many times.

JEROME KAGAN

Preface

Is Skinner correct in claiming that the popular beliefs about freedom are fictitious and misleading? Do humans actually need freedom? If freedom is a basic need, how can that fact be demonstrated? What is the nature of freedom—is it more than just a state of mind? These and allied questions stimulated the writing of this book.

My effort to answer the above questions required a study of many definitions of freedom and also of the foundations that support them. I think that the effort has been reasonably successful in showing that the Skinnerian concept of freedom is too narrow to comprehend all the nonfictitious meanings of the term. On the other hand, the common misunderstandings of Skinner's psychology, created by shoddy criticisms, have given us a measure of false security that is more serious than the uneasiness that Skinner has stimulated.

The kind of freedom that promises to be most serviceable

in the modern world is not the passive type, nor is it something that can be achieved without a special kind of effort. Skinner has done society a favor in bringing to light the questionable aspects of the popular notions of freedom, and he has forced a serious reexamination of our value system. But his analysis contains omissions that leave unrecognized the more substantial and important aspects of freedom.

Despite the knotty problems that a critical examination of freedom entails and the improbability of settling the "free-will" issue, the effort required in its study offers handsome returns. I have come to the conclusion that our future will be somewhat determined by the decisions we adopt about freedom and the actions we take thereby. If we cling to the fictions, we shall play into the hands of power seekers who aspire to establish a totalitarian system. But if we learn to value a realistic freedom and to promote its growth and distribution, the gloomy predictions of science fiction writers may be avoided.

I believe that education can play a key role in promoting the important freedoms. But it cannot do the job without support of the larger society. It seems most important to modify the popular notions of freedom and to show that the value we place in freedom need not rest on untenable assumptions.

Introduction

There is a touch of security in knowing a few statements that are absolutely free from attack. The old standbys included pronouncements against sin and those in favor of motherhood, country, and freedom. The sanctity of motherhood became slightly tinged when the danger of overpopulation was discovered. And patriotism has been more out than in, particularly among some people of draft age. Sin has little meaning today except in the shrinking pockets of fundamentalism. And now freedom, the value which Americans claim to have invented, is no longer the last vestige of safety. In a book that may become a landmark in modern history, B. F. Skinner has challenged the only remaining value that Americans hold sacred. *Beyond Freedom and Dignity* is a controversial book, but it is a signal event because no prominent American ever before had the courage and skill to place the champions of freedom on the defensive.

And now that Skinner has cast scientific doubt on the validity and usefulness of the popular interpretations of freedom, it is no longer possible to say anything with a feeling of immunity. Our quest for verbal security has ended in utter failure.

The value system upon which generations of Americans have based their life style and aspirations was a mixture of the Puritanic code, material success, and freedom. Puritanism has fallen, partly because of its friction with affluence and the rising fun culture. Freudian psychology helped to hasten the demise of Puritanism by claiming that it was too rigid for psychological health. It was convenient to heed the Freudian warning, for technology provided ample alternatives for immediate gratification. The Spartanism of the Puritanic code placed labor, duty, and sacrifice above recreation and self-indulgence. It could not survive the prosperity that it had spawned.

Material success, as a value, is still putting up a pretty good fight, but it is rusting around the edges because of the rise of a new humanism that marches under the banner of social justice. Also, the dos and don'ts publicized by ecologists tell us that material success cannot survive as a dominant value because of the growing environmental mess that the rising GNP has produced. We may be forced to relinquish our high esteem for it as a matter of collective defense.

At first glance, freedom appears to be as strong or stronger than ever. It enjoys almost total acceptance. But freedom may be in greater danger than we care to admit. The street people and their allies have tried to broaden personal freedom by attacking the establishment. The results of their efforts are dubious insofar as they include increased robustness of bureaucracy, growing demands for "law and order," and a subtle rise in centralized control. It is indeed questionable whether the obvious gains in personal freedom have offset the less obvious, but substantial, gains in new forms of control. The negative feelings that "radical liberals" have generated may comprise a mood which could, in time, create much support for Skinner's position on freedom. Even the most noble value can be brought under suspicion if it is championed by social elements held in low esteem.

Professor Skinner repudiates the popular notions of freedom. He says that while the traditional ideas of freedom have proved valuable in the past, the fictions that they contain are dysfunctional in dealing with the big problems: overpopulation, pollution, the threat of nuclear war, and crime. Skinner maintains that we must redefine freedom so that it accords with the facts of human behavior. Failure to make that adjustment and to recognize its validity might be the most costly mistake in the history of civilization. We have no alternative, according to Skinner, but to perform emergency surgery on our sick value system. Our survival depends upon it.

Skinner's book *Beyond Freedom and Dignity* was initially greeted with a wave of angry rejection. Professor Chomsky and others led an attack that had questionable validity, but rather reflected the great emotional investment that we have in freedom. After the crest of anger passed, the atmosphere was still turbulent, but a few reactions appeared that were almost rational. These later responses gave some support to Skinner's challenge, although most of them maintained substantial reservations.

Whether we like the Skinnerian position or not, it may be risky to ignore it. To label Skinner a fraud as a means of evading his thesis, as some critics have done, is to give it unwitting support. The angry reactions simply demonstrate, particularly to the pro-Skinnerians, that people behave mechanically; they are automatically turned on or off by the conditions that bear upon them. Skinner actually controlled the behavior of his critics by tossing at them a bitter morsel. It seems likely that Skinner knew all along what reaction his book would cause. While writing the book, Skinner may have knowingly said to himself, "I am going to control the behavior of many people, even some of my best friends. They will become angry and say things that are not carefully conceived because they will be under my aversive stimulus. I will cause them to think in a shoddy and defensive way. And after their heat of anger has subsided the most intelligent among them will be sheepishly aware of having displayed weaknesses that they would fain deny." I prefer to think that Skinner has not toyed deliberately with our emotions in the manner just described. But it is an attractive hypothesis when one knows the acuity and broad range of Skinner's wit.

In line with the above speculation, those who have fallen most unsuspectingly into the Skinnerian trap are the ones who have been the most vitriolic. One critic pinned an almost exhaustive supply of negative labels on Skinner and his psychology; he included such adjectives as empty, dogmatic, incoherent, fraudulent, unscientific, impoverished, and false. It is clear, however, that these adjectives do not square with the fact that Skinnerian methods are being increasingly used in such places as mental hospitals, schools for the retarded, ordinary classrooms, prisons, juvenile detention homes, military bases, industrial training schools, and the like. Whatever substantial points the angry critics have made have been buried by their efforts at overkill, which more than anything else has given Skinner the advantage in this unequal contest.

Skinner's position is vulnerable. But it cannot be challenged effectively by falling into the trap mentioned above. One must remain calm and must first have a good grasp of the Skinnerian system. Yet achieving even these obvious prerequisites is hazardous, because the emotional stimulation of Skinner's behaviorism tends to overcome rational control and because the psychology involved is less simple than it first appears. If one can resist the emotional turbulence and can probe beneath the surface, which seems, on first inspection, to comprise the whole substance of Skinner's message, he may finally get at the real content and also the short-comings of the system. In writing this book, I have made an effort to follow this strategy.

The purpose of the book is to examine Skinner's position on freedom, to acknowledge those parts which are plausible, to identify its main shortcomings, and to explore how education and freedom are related. The book has three parts. Part One is a survey of Skinnerian psychology, the foundation of the new attack on freedom. The survey includes judgments about the strengths and weaknesses of the psychology. Part One can be conveniently skipped by students of operant behaviorism, but should be helpful for those who have little grasp of the subject. My effort in dealing with Skinnerian psychology was to get across the color, spirit, and basic concepts of the system with a minimum of technical jargon. The treatment cannot be considered complete, but it should give the reader all he needs for dealing with the pros and cons of Skinnerian freedom.

Part Two first puts freedom in a wider perspective by giving a broad sample of its many meanings and pointing out its paradoxical nature along with its practical values. Then, I have examined Skinner's treatment of freedom, identifying its advantages and limitations.

Part Three begins with a discussion of three psychological freedoms, describing their nature and functions. I emphasize one freedom—cognitive freedom—that seems essential for maintaining some semblance of a working democracy. The relationships that tie together education, art, freedom, and human development are discussed in Chapter 7. Suggestions about the kind of freedom that education should uphold are given to emphasize the limitations of the Skinnerian thesis. Chapter 8 takes a critical look at my treatment of freedom and compares its probable validity with Skinner's alternative.

What kind of world would we have if we adopted the

Skinnerian plan, and applied it in such areas as child training, economics, education, and government? Chapter 9 is devoted to answering this question. Although the answer is necessarily speculative, I have tried to develop an unbiased estimate of the main features of a Skinnerian future. In the course of that development, several popular but misleading opinions on the matter are identified and rejected. The closing remarks make up a critique of the Skinner plan.

part One
THE PSYCHOLOGICAL FOUNDATIONS OF SKINNERIAN FREEDOM

CHAPTER 1

The Meaning of Skinnerian Psychology

Operant behaviorism, Skinner's psychology, is one of the most widely recognized but least understood of modern psychologies. It is hard to find a balanced treatment of it in words that the layman can understand. Skinner's books are easy to read but difficult to grasp. His notions do not flatter the human being; they are not the kinds of ideas that we like to hold about ourselves and about humans in general. Hence they often stimulate anger and other negative emotions, which do not facilitate clear understanding.

Many students and psychologists are polarized regarding operant behaviorism. The majority has a negative feeling toward it. A hardy minority defends it with a kind of smugness that is not very rewarding to others in the professional community. The dedicated Skinnerians survive under difficult conditions, but they seem to grow stronger as time passes.

3

Operant behaviorism has expanded its influence dramatically within the last decade. It has broken the monopoly long held by psychoanalysis in the field of mental therapy. It has introduced new methods of training in penal reform. It has made an impact upon education by restructuring learning materials and by using other techniques to individualize the learning process. Psychopharmacology, the study of the effect of drugs on behavior, has felt the influence of operant behaviorism. Skinner's method of experimentation, which is notable for its lack of statistical dependence and for its careful charting of changes of behavior through time, is competing with the traditional modes of experimentation that depend heavily upon statistics. The Skinnerian system has made plausible gains in dealing with delinquency, helping people break undesirable habits, and aiding retarded learners. No important area of applied psychology has escaped its impact.

The most disliked trait attributed to Skinner's disciples is a cavalier attitude toward other psychologies, an attitude that has about as much value as the poor criticisms that it arouses. Even some distinguished scholars have fallen into an unthinking denouncement of the system. Effective communication about its strengths and weaknesses in public forums and in printed symposia is infrequent. The famous debates between Skinner and Rogers were characterized by poor communication between the two, although each presented his own views quite well. (See the reference at the end of the chapter concerning those debates.) In general, the exchange of remarks between rival groups contains some of the most unscholarly interaction found in the psychological community. Consequently, it seems worthwhile to make an attempt in this book to present a dispassionate description of operant behaviorism, one that is not heavy with technical jargon.

This chapter is an outline of the psychology, with special

attention given to its dominant principle and to some fundamental beliefs on which it rests. Readers who are already acquainted with operant behaviorism can afford to skip this chapter. But for those who are confused by the arguments about it and for those who have never attempted to study it, the treatment should be helpful in following the main discussion on freedom.

THE FUNDAMENTAL MESSAGE
OF OPERANT BEHAVIORISM

All organisms, including humans, are greatly influenced by the consequences produced by their own behavior—that is the basic notion of Skinnerian psychology. Its meaning embraces the following simpler statements: (1) All animals and humans are behaving creatures. (2) A given act is followed by an experience that is a consequence of the act. (3) The quality of the consequence influences further action. An important point is that the consequence arises in the outer environment. Therefore the environment holds the key to most of the changes that occur in the way a person behaves. A few illustrations should make this notion quite clear.

A baby sitting in his high chair stretches out his arm and touches a hot iron. The consequence is a feeling of pain, along with a startled response and crying. On later occasions, when the child is within reach of the iron he *refrains* from touching it. The experienced consequence of his original act influenced him to alter his behavior toward the iron. The implication is that the baby has the ability to associate his act (touching the iron) with the experience of getting burned. The hot iron is an aversive stimulus, and any act that leads to physical contact with the hot metal is suppressed after the experience of getting burned occurs.

A toddler takes his first step toward his mother, who reacts with smiles and encouragement. The mother holds out her arms just beyond the reach of the child to stimulate him to take another step. He makes another unsteady response and reaches his mother, who hugs and kisses him. The important part of this little episode is that the child learns that he can do something to produce a positive experience. He can, in effect, control or determine his mother's reaction by initiating a certain act. The frequency of his attempting to walk increases because this act produces pleasant results. It is also quite likely that the act of walking in and of itself yields a good feeling, independent of the mother's attention and affection.

Skinner does not use the same language as I have used to account for learning. He sticks closely to concrete terms of description and to relationships that can clearly be drawn from them. He avoids such expressions as "learning occurs when the person has a pleasant feeling," because "pleasant feeling" refers to something going on inside the person that is not directly open to public view. My looser language is excusable only on the ground that it is easier to grasp because of its more common occurrence.

A child just beginning to talk can utter many babbling sounds. As the babbling proceeds, sooner or later the child says something that resembles "mamma." When the mother hears the response she suddenly beams, giving the child special attention and affection. The child is able to associate his act (saying "mamma") with the positive attention that follows it. That is a signal event in his young life. He has experienced the satisfying fact that producing a particular verbal sound has the power to bring him attention and approval from the person most significant to him. So it seems quite logical that he will attempt to repeat the word. And that is exactly what he does. Each time he says "mamma" he produces the consequence of positive attention. In a relatively short time his rate of repetition of the word is quite high. As time passes, the mother fails to express her approval each time the word is uttered. She expresses recognition of the response only occasionally. But periodic recognition is enough to keep the response at a high level of occurrence. And when a new word emerges, such as "dada," the whole episode is replayed. So the child adds new words as a means of commanding approval. Eventually the child is able to structure whole sentences, which produce reactions from others according to the meanings conveyed. He learns how to make demands, how to call attention to something in his environment or to the way he feels, and how to reinforce and punish others verbally. He becomes a competent communicator.

When the conditions of reward (reinforcement) are absent, Skinner claims that verbal learning does not occur. For example, if the baby were kept in isolation without direct contact with another human, he would probably utter sounds but would never develop a complex vocabulary and would never piece the words together to produce effective communication. While it can be argued that reinforcement is not sufficient in accounting for language learning or any other learning, it does seem to be one important condition. Skinner differs from other psychologists in assigning central importance to reward. So a proper description of reinforcing processes is virtually sufficient, in Skinnerian psychology, to account for nearly all behavior.

A student in a class contributes very little to classroom discussions. The teacher is concerned and wants to increase the student's active participation. Finally, the student asks a question. The teacher, using Skinnerian psychology, looks at the student, pauses a while, and then proceeds to comment on the good quality of the question and adds that if more questions of such quality were introduced the sessions would be more profitable to the whole class. The episode is followed by a dramatic increase in the asking of questions on the part of this student. The teacher's commendation is hence deemed reinforcing (rewarding). But for some students, approval from the teacher may act as a negative stimulus. Consequently, the art of teaching, according to Skinner, must include the identification of events that reinforce each student and the setting up of conditions that provide the opportunity for each to experience reinforcement upon making desired responses and showing progress.

A comedian collects a repertory of jokes. Those that stimulate the best audience reaction are retained for other audiences, and those that produce disappointing consequences are dropped. Thus, the repertory of jokes is literally shaped by audience reaction.

A politician campaigning for election is sensitive to public opinion. His speeches are shaped by what he thinks the public will accept and by the positive or negative responses he actually experiences. Failure to elicit positive response (e.g., with regard to the image he projects, the promises he is perceived to make, the credibility he is deemed to have) results in his either quitting the pursuit of public office or reshaping his behavior to gain greater approval.

The adolescent is much influenced by the positive and negative reactions that he gets from his teenage associates. Teenage society tends to be faddish. It creates modes of values and behavior that deviate from those of the older generation. The psychology of "in and out" plays a significant role. Certain wearing apparel, modes of speech, and forms of recreation are "in," while other kinds are "out." The average adolescent is pretty much at the mercy of the "in and out" psychology, because the approval of his peers is strongly reinforcing. His actual freedom is more apparent than real, because he usually lacks effective ways of resisting popular pressure. Canny businessmen are quick to exploit the vulnerable teenager through advertising and promotion schemes. The typical youth is usually not aware of how much he is controlled by his friends and other peers. Much of his behavior is stereotyped, but he operates under the illusion that his likes and dislikes are pretty much self-determined. Skinnerian psychology, then, is particularly descriptive of adolescent behavior.

Friendship is seen by the Skinnerian as mutual reinforcement. Friends can tolerate some criticism from one another because most of their interaction is reinforcing. But if one partner finds new friends and drifts into new patterns of behavior that are incompatible with those of his old friend, the relationship crumbles. Friendship lasts only so long as adequate reinforcement prevails. When it wanes, the ties of friendship weaken.

The above illustrations show that many acts that a person performs bring consequences which influence further action. Consequences fall into three classes: positive, negative, and neutral. The first is associated with the phenomenon of *positive reinforcement:* any act that leads to a reward or a pleasant experience (positive consequence) will increase in rate of occurrence. A negative consequence is unpleasant, harmful, or threatening and it stimulates action toward removing it. The strengthening of behavior that removes an aversive condition is called *negative reinforcement.* For example, a person who first experiences a headache and by taking an aspirin tablet succeeds in getting rid of the pain will take another aspirin upon later occurrence of a headache.

Many acts produce neutral results; they bring neither reward nor punishment. Such acts are not psychologically significant because they produce no consequences that have any strong influence on changing behavior. However, if an act has been consistently followed by a reward in the past, but fails to result in the expected reward, frustration occurs. And if many repetitions of the act fail to result in the expected reward, the act will grow less and less frequent and will eventually become extinguished.

The sum and substance of Skinnerian psychology is that rewards, threats, and punishments shape the patterns of behavior that make up human personalities. And the most important fact is that a person's own behavior brings consequences that change his action. In addition, consequences arise in the environment; hence, the environment influences or controls changes in behavior. All acts are performed in some environmental setting. Even daydreaming, imagining, speculating, and the like occur in some context. When they are transformed into concrete action, they produce consequences in the physical world.

 The second major notion of Skinnerian psychology is closely related to the one just described, and it is so central that it must be clearly grasped before any sense can be made of the psychology. This is the concept of "contingency." It is used in speaking about behavior and the consequences produced by behavior, and refers to the proposition that a reward can occur only if some act precedes it. Animals and humans are continually doing something: seeing, listening, feeling, and moving about. They do things that trigger the environment to react. For example, a phone call in a pay booth cannot be completed unless one makes the necessary movements in putting the proper coin in a slot. Completing the call is *contingent upon* inserting the coin. People and animals are sensitive to the sequencing of events. They are able to associate their action with certain consequences. A cat must approach a food dish before it can eat the food in the dish. It must bring its mouth into contact with the food, grasp some portion at a time, chew, and swallow. The rewarding value of the food depends or is contingent upon a series of responses that precedes ingestion. People learn many patterns of response that are instrumental in producing rewards. So a contingency of reinforcement is a sequence of events in which some key act is necessary before the reward can be experienced. A contingency of reinforcement is basically a probability statement. It means that if a certain act is performed, the probability of a reward becomes greatly increased. Hence, a contingency of reinforcement means that a key response is necessary but not always sufficient to produce reward.

The idea of contingency may become a little clearer if one imagines that the environment engages in a trade-off game with the animal or human, yielding a reinforcer only after the person behaves a certain way. Skinner regards contingencies as necessary in making reliable descriptive accounts of human and animal behavior. Several examples of contingency should help you to enter this frame of reference of operant behaviorism.

A vending machine will relinquish the item of your choice only after you place the correct number of coins in a certain slot. Obtaining the article you desire (the reinforcer) is made contingent upon a certain act. Although the machine may fail to work as expected on some occasions, it virtually never yields merchandise *unless* the right amount of change is fed into it.

Getting an "A" in school without cheating depends upon a certain level of performance as perceived by the teacher. Top achievement is reinforced by a top grade. Poor performance yields a poor evaluation.

Going from one place to another in a car depends upon how the driver controls the vehicle. Inappropriate and dysfunctional operations increase the chance of having a wreck. Reinforcement for adequate driving is a safe arrival at one's destination. (Note the trade-off function in this and other examples. The environment yields a certain outcome only if certain behavior occurs.)

If one belittles another person, the second person is likely to do one of two things: retaliate (give tit for tat) or simply withdraw and avoid further contact with the critic.

If a motorist travels through a red light at an intersection, the consequences are likely to be punishing, particularly if the event is spotted by a traffic policeman. The ticket issued to the violator is punishing because it delays the motorist, results in a fine, and may produce an increased insurance premium.

A person who smiles and displays a friendly attitude toward others is likely to stimulate them to react in a friendly manner. Gruff and insolent behavior usually brings negative reactions.

A thirsty person is reinforced by a cold drink of water. But before he receives the reward he must perform a certain pattern of behavior: he must approach the source of water, bring his mouth in contact with it, and perform a swallowing act. So even the quenching of thirst and hunger depends upon chains of instrumental responses.

Before one succeeds in getting a desired job, he usually must behave a certain way toward the employer. His background and record of relevant experience are examined. Assessments are made of the perceived personality traits and habits of the candidate and judgments rendered as to whether or not these traits are compatible with the job. The decision to hire the applicant is usually determined by the promise that he shows of reinforcing the employer in quite specific ways.

The selection of a spouse boils down to judgments about the reinforcing powers of a candidate. Few marriages occur in our culture without mutual evaluation made by the principals. While judgments that lead to marriage often turn out to be wrong, they are always made with an eye to evidence that promises rewarding experiences. This goes under such labels as "good looks," "congeniality," "sexiness," "material assets," "shared interests and activities," and so on.

Fundamentally, Skinner's psychology is a psychology of values. Positive values are assigned to those events that are rewarding, while negative values emerge from experiences that bring aversive stimulation. The human is a value-making creature in the sense that his own behavior produces results that are sorted into positive and negative effects. If we asked Skinner why the human is a value-making creature, his response would probably be "Natural Selection": that is, only those people survive to produce their own kind who are sensitive to the important consequences of their own behavior.

A given marriage survives to the extent that the partners can make sensitive evaluations about how to behave to sustain mutual reinforcement. When mutual reinforcement fades and is replaced by aversive interactions, the partners tend to avoid one another and they often seek escape via divorce. The growing doubts about the value of marriage are based on the estimate that marriage typically produces a greater balance of aversive results than of rewarding ones. But Skinnerian psychology implies that conditions can be so managed in a marriage that the rewards far outweigh the unpleasant consequences. Therefore, one should not look upon marriage as essentially good or bad per se, but it should be seen as something that requires proper management. People should be trained in the skills that produce and sustain mutual reinforcement in marriage. Many of the usual kinds of advice for sick marriages fail to deal with the specific behavioral interactions that yield important consequences. The advice is often one-sided and fails to identify and describe the managerial details necessary for adequate results.

The influential aspects of religion are comprised in the contingencies of reinforcement and punishment found in its tenets. Religion is quite practical because it stipulates the dos and don'ts of everyday living. The commandment "Thou shalt not kill" clearly implies that if one violates it aversive consequences will result. After one has been conditioned to accept this rule of conduct, it serves as a powerful stimulus for shaping certain behavior. Moral precepts found in religious doctrines are simply practical guidelines outlining contingencies that have produced desirable outcomes. When moral precepts are attributed to a superior being they take on added power, because within such a belief system there is no way to escape divine evaluation.

In theory, Skinner's psychology supports religion, regardless of whatever religious beliefs that Skinner, himself, may have. Insofar as a religion helps to sensitize a person to useful contingencies, it is good despite whatever theological weaknesses it may have. The interesting implication of these considerations is that it makes no practical difference whether or not a doctrine is fundamentally true; the important thing is how it influences the person to behave. The basic assumptions of religion transcend the realm of demonstrable truth and falsity, because they cannot be evaluated in the same way as a scientific proposition. Hence it seems inappropriate to analyze articles of religious faith on logical grounds. The final assessment of any religion must, for a Skinnerian, be based on its behavioral influence. A religion completely devoid of any promises of reward or punishment made contingent upon how one behaves cannot be called a "religion" in the operant context.

Civil laws can be couched in terms of contingencies of punishment. For example, the income-tax law says in effect that if one fails to submit a tax return or fails to pay the due amount, aversive consequences will occur. Therefore, what one fails to do can bring bad consequences. The legal structure serves as a threat system insofar as it contains laws which promise punishment for acts of either omission or commission. Skinner seems to think that too many civil laws threaten punishment and too few promise reward. He would like to see a system that ensures efficient shaping of moral behavior with little or no dependence upon laws of a threatening nature.

An operant analysis of laws, codes, customs, and other social rules reduces them to contingencies of reinforcement and punishment. If they could not be so reduced, they would amount to empty expressions having no psychological impact. Some laws are ineffective because they are so ambiguous that even legal experts are confused about just what behavior constitutes a violation.

So far, the main points of operant psychology boil down to just three propositions: (1) what a person does often has consequences that alter his behavior, (2) the consequences arise in the environment, and (3) the environment operates on a contingency basis; that is, it yields rewards only after certain acts are performed. The environment also contains unpleasant or punishing potentials, which are activated on a contingency basis. These assertions imply that a person has the ability to associate his behavior with the consequences that are experienced. In addition, there is some genetic or built-in tendency to sort consequences into "good" and "bad" classes that are generally associated with survival. An organism avoids noxious conditions because it is genetically wired to sustain its physical safety. Good consequences are those that meet the needs of survival and growth. Skinner avoids using the concept of "need" as I have just used it, because he thinks that it is unnecessary. But it is a helpful notion for grasping the connection between reinforcement and survival.

OTHER IMPORTANT PROPOSITIONS

Every psychological theory or system rests on a set of relevant beliefs held by the theory maker. The beliefs are not a part of the technical concepts and principles that make up the working heart of the theory, but understanding them is quite important for grasping the spirit and essential flavor of the theory. The following sample of notions held by Skinner are of this kind.

1. There exists a set of systematic and functional relation-

ships between the behavior of an organism and the environment.

2. The discovery of these relationships is necessary before a useful science of behavior can be developed.

3. Psychological data should represent events about which independent observers can agree. Agreement should exist on the observable properties of the events.

4. It is unnecessary and even misleading to speculate on what is happening beneath the skin in order to explain behavior, unless the psychologist is equipped to make the necessary observations to test the truthfulness of his guesses. But because the psychologist usually makes no observations of events beneath the skin, his guesses about them remain unverified and therefore any inaccuracies in his untested guesses will serve to maintain basic errors of interpretation. Biological processes occurring inside the skin are no doubt important, but fortunately a science of behavior can be built without referring to them because the organism behaves in a systematic way according to the environmental consequences of its own behavior.

5. A science of behavior ought to be developed inductively—that is, it should be constructed by first observing behavior and then identifying the relationships between patterns of responses and environmental conditions. Inductive generalizations have a more substantial basis than purely hypothetical postulates. Deductive systems that begin with speculative principles tend to be cumbersome and they dispose the psychologist to "theory-tinkering," resulting in loss of attention to available facts.

6. Organisms belonging to different species share some basic similarities. Therefore, the most generic principles of behavior apply to all species. This does not mean that humans and rats are identical; it simply means that rats and humans share certain psychological tendencies, just as they share physiological similarities.

7. A relevant science of human behavior generates a technology that is useful for dealing with a wide variety of practical problems.

8. The organism is capable of multiple forms of action in most situations. His physical structure allows for a wide range of possible behavior.

9. Overt behavior of the person has some impact upon the environment. The impact varies with the kind and strength of the response.

Skinner's criticisms of other systems are related to one or more of the above points. He believes that when a theorist ignores these propositions he is likely to build a system that may generate much interesting talk but will be weak in application value.

CENTRAL CONCEPTS AND PRINCIPLES OF OPERANT BEHAVIORISM

Many books and articles contain the technical concepts of the psychology. I shall not try to cover the entire set; only the major principles and concepts will be mentioned. The reader is referred to the numerous books on learning theories for a more complete description. However, the technical heart of the system will be treated so that the newcomer may grasp the basic working propositions of Skinnerian psychology.

REINFORCEMENT

As mentioned before, reinforcement is roughly equivalent to reward. The principle of reinforcement can be stated as follows: *When a given act is followed closely by a reinforcer (reward), the organism tends to increase the frequency of that act under the same or similar conditions.* Any act or chain of acts is established in the repertory of an organism's behavior only by some form of reinforcement, either positive or negative. Therefore, any pattern of behavior that occurs frequently must automatically have been reinforced.

POSITIVE REINFORCEMENT

When an animal or person does something that results in the presentation of a positive stimulus, such as food, water, sexual contact, approval, praise, and the like, and when evidence of the principle of reinforcement is manifested, the process is called *positive reinforcement*.

NEGATIVE REINFORCEMENT

Any act that is successful in removing an aversive stimulus (roughly, one that is uncomfortable, noxious, or in some way negative) will increase in frequency when the same or a similar aversive stimulus is later experienced. It is important to note that negative reinforcement is not the same as punishment, with which it is often confused. In simpler language, a person learns that he can escape from an uncomfortable situation by performing some act. Any such act will be *strengthened*—that is, it will occur with increasing frequency as a means of escaping the aversive stimulus. Both positive and negative reinforcement, therefore, strengthen the associated behavior.

OPERANT BEHAVIOR

Animals and humans are dynamic creatures. They move about in space and encounter a great variety of environmental stimuli. It is impossible to determine exactly what stimulus or set of stimuli gives rise to each and every act. Therefore, a great deal of behavior occurs without an observer's being able to determine just what stimuli predispose it. Operant behavior, then, is that which is roughly, but not technically, equivalent to voluntary behavior. Skinner's system stresses the importance of operant behavior, which makes up most of the everyday activity that animals and humans exhibit. The main thrust of his psychology is to study operant behavior and to describe its systematic changes as certain environmental conditions are changed. Skinner begins with the behaving organism and tries to identify relationships between changes in the frequency of specific acts and alteration of certain conditions in the environment. His concept of reinforcement and allied principles are supplied as evidence that a science of behavior is possible simply by noting how behavior is modified in relation to environmental feedback.

DIFFERENTIAL REINFORCEMENT

This notion is used to account for the development of special skills such as typing, playing the piano, mastering games, and the many patterns of acts that comprise successful work by auto mechanics, plumbers, bricklayers, and so on. Such skills are acquired by learning *how* to perform acts so as to maximize their practical value. For example, learning how to pitch a curve ball in the game of baseball involves the learning of a correct chain of responses including the proper grip on the ball, a special way of releasing the ball, and so on. Simply throwing the ball in the ordinary way will probably not produce a curve. As the pitcher follows the cues of his coach and a curve is produced by a given pattern of responses, skilled performance tends to become established. Usually, skill learning requires considerable practice, because the minute variations in how an act can be performed are quite numerous; the skill learner must practice until he masters the delicate sequence of responses that produces maximum success.

In learning a skill, the person must be able to observe

immediately the results of his efforts, so that he can be guided by effective feedback as to how to alter his manner of performance. Differential reinforcement occurs when small shifts in how an act is performed produce quite different results. For example, a beginning golfer may hold his club so that the head of the club is turned slightly outward rather than perpendicular to the line toward the target. When the error is called to his attention and he makes the proper adjustment, his effort becomes vastly more successful. Thus, slight changes in a pattern of performance can produce great differences in outcomes, the learner is able to associate such small changes in performance with improved results. And those results which are most successful will strengthen the behavior that produces them. Hence, success in skill learning depends upon the differential consequences produced by one's actions.

Education tries to promote many skills via differential reinforcement, such as effective grammar, effective communication (both written and oral), and various kinds of shop work.

SUCCESSIVE APPROXIMATIONS

Skinner maintains that behavior can be shaped; that is, by means of controlling conditions any given pattern of behavior within the capabilities of the person can be established. Some of the most dramatic illustrations of his claim were afforded by experiments with pigeons. For example, it was decided to teach pigeons to bowl. The ball was an ordinary marble. The object of the effort was to shape the pigeon's behavior so that it would approach the marble and give it a sharp sweep with its beak in the direction of a set of pins. Bowling simply does not exist in the repertory of behavior of untrained pigeons, so this pattern of behavior is quite unique and calls for radical changes in the way pigeons behave. But bowling is a realistic objective, because the pigeon has considerable strength and flexibility of movement in its beak. The problem that faced Skinner was: how should conditions be managed so as to establish the behavior of bowling? He could not expect that the pigeon would step up to the marble and give it a proper stroke upon the first trial. Skinner had to predispose the pigeon to address the ball, hit it, and make a stroke so that the ball would go in the proper direction. Such expectations seem excessive when applied to a pigeon. But the stroke of genius that occurred to one of Skinner's colleagues was the simple, but effective, principle of reinforcing the pigeon with a grain of food each time it happened to more closely *approximate* the desired pattern of behavior. So at first the pigeon was reinforced simply for looking at the marble, then for approaching it, then for pecking it, and so on. Reinforcement was withheld when the pigeon regressed, i.e., returned to a less desirable pattern of behavior. In a relatively short time, the pigeon exhibited the behavior of a skillful bowler, insofar as the pigeon's physique allowed. Pigeons were also taught by this method of *successive approximations* to walk special patterns such as a figure 8, to peck discs in a certain sequence so to produce simple tunes, to play table tennis, and the like. So shaping occurs gradually by reinforcing small improvements and withholding reward for undesirable digressive behavior.

When applied to human behavior, successive approximations can be detected in programmed instruction and in the use of tokens to establish patterns of social behavior in schools, mental hospitals, prisons, and other settings.

OPERANT DISCRIMINATION

Humans and many animals are equipped with multiple senses, ability to see, hear, smell, feel, taste, a sense of balance, and others. They can distinguish various forms, colors, textures, and odors. *Operant discrimination* is possible because of these sensitivities. The principle of operant discrimination can be stated as follows: when a response is rewarded only in the presence of a key stimulus and is not rewarded when that key stimulus is absent, the organism learns to perform the response only when that stimulus is present. The key stimulus is called the *discriminant stimulus*. For example, a rat can readily be conditioned to press a lever to produce a bit of food. But suppose that after the rat has learned this behavior, a change in conditions is introduced, so that the rat is rewarded for pressing the lever only when a light is on and no reward is given for the response when the light is off. Consistent use of this rule will result in the expected change—namely, the rat will press the lever only when the light is on. The light in this case is the discriminant stimulus.

Human behavior reflects many instances of operant discrimination. When one is driving, for example, a red traffic light is the discriminant stimulus for pushing the brake pedal. The reinforcement is avoidance of a mishap. The sounding of a fire alarm in a school is a stimulus that triggers an orderly and safe exit. The reinforcement is avoidance of panic and the serious accidents that could result therefrom. A memo book is used by an executive as a reminder to attend important meetings. A person preparing notes for a conference will consult his watch to regulate his pace and give him information about when he should depart to meet his appointment. A driver on a trip looks at his gasoline gauge and notices that it registers almost empty. The reading is a stimulus for looking around for signs of the nearest service station. Reinforcement is obtained when the driver reaches a station before exhausting his fuel supply. When a popular speaker rises to address an audience, his behavior just prior to speaking serves to stimulate attention and evoke a quiet atmosphere so as to allow for a clear reception of his message. In general, the environment contains many objects and events that serve as discriminative stimuli to trigger certain acts so as to produce expected reinforcers.

PUNISHMENT

Technically, punishment occurs in two forms: when a given act is followed by the presentation of an aversive stimulus, and when an act is followed by the *removal* of a positive stimulus. An example of the first kind of punishment is when a mother spanks her child for bad conduct. The second kind of punishment is manifested by depriving the child of something he values because he performed an undesirable act. The mother may refuse to let her boy play ball because of his coming home late from school.

Although punishment can be used to control behavior, Skinner believes that its use is generally inefficient. He thinks that any society is improved by shifting from a threat system to an effective use of reinforcers. The trouble with punishment is that its desirable effects are often of short duration, while its undesirable effects may be quite lasting. For example, the use of threat and punishment by a teacher to achieve classroom discipline works only while the teacher is physically present. When she steps from the room, bedlam often breaks loose, indicating that control by punishment does not lessen the tendency to commit certain acts, but only suppresses it while the agent of punishment is present. So it takes much surveillance to sustain the effectiveness of a threat system. The bad and lasting effects of punishment may include the development of excessive timidity and anxiety, and lack of adventure and spontaneity.

Skinner believes that the social environment should be relatively free from dependence upon punishment as a means of control. But simply to be free from social punishment does not mean that the person is free from all control. Indeed, the most effective control is by positive reinforcement, and Skinner claims that its ethical use is the best means for producing a happy and productive society.

ENVIRONMENTAL CONTROL

Skinner sees the environment as exerting great control over the person's behavior because the consequences produced by one's action arise *in* the environment. Also, the environment contains all the vital elements on which life depends. The environment on the moon cannot sustain human life because of extreme temperatures and the lack of oxygen, water, food, and atmospheric pressure. Before astronauts can function on the moon they must carry a supporting environment with them. A baby must be nurtured by an adequate environment in order to survive. Food must come from external sources, and a caring person (part of the infant's environment) must act to meet the needs of the child.

All action takes place in some setting. The way a person behaves in a given environment pretty much determines how that environment reacts, particularly if it includes other people. A person who flouts all the rules practiced in a community will evoke on aversive reaction from others. His position becomes socially untenable, and the reinforcement that normally comes from others is cut off; he becomes a social isolate and hence cannot function as an acceptable member of the community. A criminal has not been imprisoned because of what he thinks, nor on the basis of what he feels, imagines, or wishes. He is jailed because of his *behavior*, acts that are deemed intolerable by others. So the consequences that his own behavior produces are determined by how his behavior affects other people. The essence of social maturation is the acquisition of the art of reinforcing other people without compromising one's own position excessively. Love—which involves reinforcing others with sincerity—is mutually reinforcing because a person is willing to sacrifice his own convenience for the benefit of others. His reinforcement lies in the realization that his acts of consideration are valued within the social belief system.

No act can be performed independent of some context. The meaning of any act depends upon how it relates to the context, what consequences it produces. If one becomes so blasé that he deems nothing to have any significance, it simply means that he has either reached a point of satiation or that his efforts to achieve reinforcement have been habitually thwarted and so he regards any effort as futile. An attitude of nihilism arises from the consequences that one's own behavior produces. And the same is true for attitudes of optimism and hope. No attitude, philosophy, feeling, belief, or habit pattern occurs *de novo*. All such states arise from interaction between the person and his environment. No human experience can be divorced from some environmental context. The importance and influence of the environment cannot be exaggerated.

SELF-CONTROL

If the environment controls the person, how can self-control have any meaning? Skinner allows for the notion that the person has the ability to manipulate certain environmental variables, which in turn control his behavior. For example, a person can learn how to budget and use money effectively rather than waste it. Yet money, in turn, influences a significant portion of his action. One works for money because he can use it to gain a variety of other reinforcers—food, housing, clothing, services, luxuries. Some people carefully control money so as to maximize its positive consequences. Others waste it and become excessively indebted. Similarly, a successful student acquires effective study habits, which amount to efficient ways of, for example, budgeting time, locating and manipulating sources of information, filing notes for ready reference, and managing a study environment so as to minimize noise and other distractions. An overweight person desires to be slender. He may join Weight Watchers and learn how to select and prepare dishes that are both satisfying and low in calories. He is able to identify the kind of behavior to be controlled, and then takes steps to control those variables that in turn control his behavior.

The above illustrations may appear to undercut the main thesis of Skinnerian psychology, namely, the notion that outer conditions rather than internal powers determine one's behavior. But Skinner does not abandon the principle of environmental control in recognizing the existence of self-control. He makes environmental control and self-control compatible by saying that the latter is simply a subclass of the former. For example, an overweight person *wants* to lose weight, and this enables him to exercise self-control. But Skinner claims that the desire to lose weight, though it seems to originate in the mind of the person, is actually determined by the social environment. The person has been treated by others so as to believe or think that being overweight is aversive, that too much fat is ugly, unhealthy, and prevents the experiencing of many rewarding events. In other cultures, obesity is looked upon as desirable, and hence is associated with a variety of social reinforcers. So the desire to lose or gain weight does not arise from a perfectly free decision of the person, but is conditioned by the social community. In our culture, then, losing excessive weight is related to an increase in social reinforcement and a reduction of aversive social reactions. The behavior that leads to weight reduction amounts to a manipulation of variables producing escape from an unpleasant state. Hence, both positive and negative reinforcement are involved in the

process of losing weight, as in the breaking of many undesirable habits.

SCHEDULES OF REINFORCEMENT

The environment manifests different patterns of yielding
rewards. Under some conditions a reward occurs each time
a certain response is emitted. For example, in using a type-
writer, every time an intended key is punched the expected
letter is typed. A well-stocked vending machine in good
working order will dispense the wanted article after each
correct response pattern. A tuned car engine will start
nearly every time the starter is properly engaged. A large
shade tree will shield one from the hot sun every time one
moves within its shadow. When there is a one-to-one relation between the occurrence of a key response and a rewarding result, the schedule of reinforcement is said to be
continuous. The physical environment, both natural and man-
made, tends to be rather stable or consistent. Hence, continuous reinforcement is more likely to occur in a setting of
things than in a social context.

Such devices as telephones, TV sets, lamps, refrigerators,
can openers, electric coffee makers, hair dryers, washing
machines, automobiles, blenders, electric stoves, fans, computers, and many other gadgets are usually so dependable
that we expect them to function properly each time we
operate them. They have been engineered to be consistent.
When they fail to function properly we get them repaired
so that they will perform as expected. Also, much of the
natural environment, excluding animals and other people,
tends to be highly consistent. Such consistency yields continuous reinforcement.

The psychological impact of the continuous schedule of
reinforcement is significant. Skinner has clearly demonstrated that animals trained on a continuous schedule ex-

hibit certain psychological features, perhaps the most important being low frustration tolerance. A rat, for example, that has received food each time he presses a bar will show visible signs of frustration or what we call "emotional unrest" when bar pressing fails to deliver the expected reward. Such a rat also tends to give up easily (that is, it will quickly lose its tendency to press the bar); it has relatively weak perseverance or stick-to-itiveness. It is not equipped to endure hard times.

In middle-class American society it is possible that too much reinforcement occurs in nurturing children. Operant behaviorism sees parents as indulgent if they reward their children too frequently and under conditions that require little productive effort on the part of the child. By so doing, such parents fail to condition perseverance and tend to produce such features in their children as impatience, lack of industriousness, giving up too easily under challenging conditions, impulsiveness, and low frustration tolerance. The conveniences provided by technological gadgets work in concert with parental indulgence by providing immediate gratification with great consistency while requiring little effort. Coke machines, television sets, automobiles, and many other devices yield rewards quickly and consistently with a minimum of sweat. Indulgent parents, who readily provide their children the means for making life easy and convenient, should not be surprised to find that their children lack some of the old-fashioned traits that the parents were taught to admire in their early lives.

Skinner thinks that human personality is composed of acquired patterns of behavior, established by the interaction between the person and his environment. A person has multiple selves. The self which he displays with a gang of peers is not the same as he may display at home, at church, or under other social conditions. The self that he manifests at any given time pretty much depends on the conditions that surround him.

The second major pattern of reinforcement is called *intermittent reinforcement.* It means that a given reward does not occur every time an appropriate act is emitted. The social environment, except for the indulgent parent, tends to reward a given person's action in an uneven or irregular manner. In other words, it is often hard to predict just when some rewards will occur. People are dynamic and somewhat inconsistent, and they are subjected to a multitude of stimulating conditions. They are not constituted to react with the consistency that is found in machines engineered for maximum reliability. People tend to reinforce and punish one another in irregular ways.

Intermittent reinforcement has a variety of forms, and each form has one or more psychological effects. The *fixed-ratio schedule* of reward is one in which a single reward is given for a fixed number of responses. A rat trained to press a bar on a continuous schedule can be shifted to a fixed-ratio schedule by presenting food after a fixed number of responses occur. For example, a rat might be rewarded only after every third response, every fifth response, etc.; as the ratio is gradually shifted upward, the amount of work required for each reward increases accordingly. The psychological impact of the fixed-ratio schedule is an increase in persistence, the tendency to emit a high rate of response over long periods of time. Rats trained under fixed-ratio schedules will continue to work much longer than rats trained under the continuous schedule *after* reinforcement is permanently withheld. We label the same tendency in people by the term "perseverance." Piecework pay in industry reflects the fixed-ratio notion. Transient laborers who harvest crops are often paid a fixed amount for each basket of fruit or carton of vegetables picked. Since pay is contingent on the amount of work done, the workers tend to perform with considerable speed and accuracy. But unfortunately the fixed-ratio schedule can be arbitrarily changed by the employer and shifted to a ratio that exploits the workers. Labor unions have succeeded in reducing the use of piecework by a threat system involving strikes. When used judiciously, piecework pay serves to maintain high productivity while yielding good wages. But because many employers have used it to get maximum profit at the expense of labor, piecework pay has been reduced by the action of unions.

The *variable-ratio schedule* presents rewards on an irregular basis. The amount of work required per reinforcement varies somewhat randomly within certain limits. A rat, for example, that is put on a variable-ratio schedule will receive food pellets on an *average* of so many responses per reward. But the distribution of the rewards is irregular, so that the exact time of occurrence of a given reward is uncertain. The variable-ratio schedule produces even greater perseverance than the fixed-ratio schedule. For example, a slot machine yields returns on an irregular basis. The reward is contingent upon feeding the machine with coins and pulling the lever. Most gambling games are based on the variable-ratio schedule and they often gain considerable control over those who engage in them.

The remaining two schedules, which will be only briefly treated here, are the *fixed-interval* and the *variable-interval* schedules. The *fixed-interval schedule* provides a payoff at fixed times. For example, a worker on salary is paid at fixed intervals. His work is not completely controlled by the salary because of the existence of many other conditions in the job environment. Yet given the choice between two salaries, one much greater than the other, most people will choose the larger one if other conditions are reasonably comparable. When animals are placed under the fixed-interval schedule in controlled environments, their rate of response is low immediately after a payoff and rises increasingly until the next reward. So under the fixed-interval schedule work output does not remain constant. The effect on human behavior is probably comparable, but other factors usually complicate an accurate assessment under every-day conditions.

The *variable-interval schedule* is an irregular payoff series based on time instead of work output. An average number of rewards is dispensed over a given time period, but within that period rewards are dispensed unevenly. The effect is a high and consistent rate of responding, including strong persistence of responding over lengthy period of no reward.

Reinforcement schedules have a great deal to do with response strength, that is, the extent to which a response is repeated without being reinforced. The intermittent schedules bring about much greater response strength than the continuous schedule. Psychologically, response strength is a basic ingredient of such personality traits as perseverance, courage, frustration tolerance, dependability, industriousness, consistency, honesty, loyalty, vigilance, and trustworthiness. These traits are traditionally seen as virtues because they result in behavior patterns that are rather stable and reinforcing to others. People who behave in a relatively consistent fashion form a social environment that is easier to adjust to than one composed of persons who are flighty, impulsive, undependable, and the like. In other words, a person having strong patterns of behavior is more predictable than one having weak patterns.

A human virtue seems to boil down to strong patterns of behavior that serve to reinforce others in a dependable way, although the circumstances may make the reinforcing act difficult to perform. The virtue called "love," for example, is fundamentally a set of acts that reflect self-sacrifice in bringing benefits to others. The response patterns must be strong; hence, they depend upon a history of intermittent reinforcement.

In summary, the continuous schedule is important in *acquiring* new behavior. But the intermittent schedules are necessary for building response *strength*. A good social environment is one which promotes the establishment of behavior that is mutually beneficial to the individual and his associates, and uses intermittent schedules to strengthen such behavior so that its effects can be somewhat consistent and dependable. Also, a good social environment leaves aversive and noxious patterns unrewarded.

The dream that Skinner entertains is to convince others to accept the thesis that cultural improvement is now within our grasp and that we can realize it only if we are willing to use the technology of behavioral engineering. We can no longer afford to ignore the controlling environment; we must adopt a program that results in systematic control over those conditions that shape the behavior of people. We can remake society on a much better level if we use the tools of the science of behavior to extinguish crime, war, and pollution, all of which are caused by how people behave. We now have the power to influence virtually all people to acquire the human virtues and to minimize those behaviors called vices. When the virtues prevail and the vices are extinguished we shall no longer find it necessary to pay so much lip service to extolling humaneness and deploring vice.

SUMMARY OF KEY TERMS

A brief review of key technical concepts is provided below so that the reader can have a handy reference with which to refresh his memory in dealing with later sections.

Operant behavior—Approximates "voluntary behavior" and serves to operate on the environment, producing consequences that influence further action.

Reinforcement—The central principle of learning that refers to the fact that an act becomes more frequent when it is followed by a positive consequence.

Differential reinforcement—Occurrence of reward that is related to *how* an act is performed. Quite frequently, very slight changes in performance spell the difference between strong reward and none at all. The *way* a golfer uses his club determines the difference, for example, between a good and a poor shot.

Successive approximations—A gradual shaping of behavior that occurs through reinforcing slight improvements until the desired pattern is achieved.

Operant discrimination—An act triggered by a signal or key stimulus. It results from a conditioning process in which reward follows a given response only when that response occurs during the presence of the signal (discriminant stimulus).

Punishment—Any aversive consequence that follows a given act.

Environmental control—The influence of outer conditions on behavior, due to the fact that the environment is the source of all reinforcers (rewards). The environment yields rewards on a contingency basis and hence determines one's repertory of responses.

Self-control—The process of manipulating conditions that in turn have an influence on behavior. The manipulation is done in such a way that desirable outcomes become more probable while undesirable consequences tend to become less frequent.

Continuous reinforcement—A schedule of reward in which a reinforcement follows the occurrence of each key response.

Intermittent reinforcement—Any schedule of reward that is not continuous; only *some* of the key responses are rewarded. Intermittent schedules tend to increase frustration tolerance, perseverance, and patience and to lower impulsiveness. They increase *response strength*—that is, the extent to which a response will be repeated when reward is scarce.

Fixed-ratio schedule of reinforcement—An intermittent schedule of reward that requires a fixed number of responses before one reinforcer is delivered. The ratio can be gradually increased until a large amount of work precedes each reward.

Variable-ratio schedule of reinforcement—An intermittent schedule in which reward occurs at intervals which are unpredictable, but which average out in the long run to equal so many responses per reward. Its significant feature is that the occurrence of any given reward cannot be accurately predicted. Such a feature tends to make learned responses become quite strong.

Fixed-interval schedule reinforcement—An intermittent schedule in which rewards occur at fixed points in time.

Variable-interval schedule of reinforcement—Similar to the fixed-interval schedule except that rewards occur somewhat randomly within a given time period. It differs from the variable-ratio schedule in that it is controlled by time instead of by the number of responses.

Contingency of reinforcement—This refers to the environmental conditions that control the occurrence of rewards. A reward is contingent upon a response when the emision of that response greatly increases the chance that a reward will occur. Certainty is ruled out, but under some conditions a given response is almost certain to produce reinforcement.

How valid is Skinnerian psychology? What are its basic strengths and weaknesses? The next chapter is an attempt to answer these questions. It will begin by identifying several popular misconceptions of operant behaviorism.

FOR FURTHER READING

ROGERS, CARL R., and SKINNER, B. F. "Some Issues Concerning the Control of Human Behavior: A Symposium." *Science* 124 (1956): 1057–1066.

SKINNER, B. F. *The Behavior of Organisms.* New York: Appleton-Century-Crofts, 1938.

———. *Cumulative Record.* New York: Appleton-Century-Crofts, 1959.

———. *Science and Human Behavior.* New York: Macmillan Company, 1953.

———. *The Technology of Teaching.* New York: Appleton-Century-Crofts, 1968.

———. *Verbal Behavior.* New York: Appleton-Century-Crofts, 1957.

CHAPTER 2

Strengths and Weaknesses of Skinnerian Psychology

The science of psychology embraces a number of theories and techniques which seek to describe and account for the emotional, mental, and behavioral nature of human beings. While there is some agreement across the different psychologies, there is also considerable disagreement, partly because the originators of the various theories adopt different approaches, accept different assumptions, and assign different values to existing problems and methods. Despite much research, psychology remains an uncoordinated field of diverse ideologies, theories, and methods. The kind of ferment needed to create a reasonably unified discipline is still awaited. The same immature status applies to all the other social sciences.

Within the above state of affairs, operant behaviorism is one of a number of systems vying for acceptance and survival. We should not be surprised to discover that operant behaviorism and other psychologies have been misunderstood and poorly evaluated, and that they have been expected to yield results foreign to their intent and nature. It is worthwhile to recognize some of the popular but incorrect opinions about Skinnerian psychology, so that the air can be cleared for concentration on the more substantial and relevant aspects of the system.

POPULAR MISCONCEPTIONS

The following criticisms have been frequently applied to operant behaviorism. Each criticism is sufficiently weak to merit rejection.

SKINNER CASTS THE HUMAN IN THE IMAGE OF THE MACHINE

Some time ago Skinner wrote the following: "It is neither plausible nor expedient to conceive of the organism as a complicated jack-in-the-box with a long list of tricks, each of which may be evoked by pressing the proper button." The notion of operant behavior is roughly equivalent to that of voluntary action, which is emitted by the person without knowledge of causal stimuli. Skinner thinks that it is impossible to identify all the causes that presumably give rise to an operant response. If that is accepted, there is certainly room for freedom in the system, although Skinner prefers to *assume* that behavior is determined. But if it is not possible to identify the causes of some behavior, it is logical to think that indeterminism can be introduced without contradicting what is known. Operant behavior implies that the organism generates energy that is translated into behavior. The theory does not include any description of mechanistic functions that account for how energy gives rise to any particular act.

To accept the assumption that behavior is determined does not necessarily mean that man is a mere machine. Instead of arguing that man is constructed to agree with the machine model, Skinner turns this assertion around. He says that machines are made to approximate certain human functions. The human is the prototype and machines are rough copies of some human attributes. Skinner's switch is interesting because it provides a realistic perspective of the evolution of the machine. It agrees with the notion that machines extend the range of human capabilities. The simple lever, for example, extends the range of human physical strength.

As the machine continues to evolve it becomes more complicated and it tends to behave in a more humanlike manner. Science fiction, which sometimes provides predictions of astonishing accuracy, has long ago described machines that rival and surpass humans in virtually all respects. As robots are produced to simulate more and more human functions, it becomes increasingly clear that it is the machine that is modeled on the human and not the other way around.

Operant behaviorism holds that what an organism does is related to its structure and to outer conditions. When and if machines can perform the range of human activities in the areas of doing, thinking, and feeling, the legal, social and political complications involving the two species may become quite acute. Machines already outstrip man's muscle power, and computers can solve certain problems with a speed and accuracy that exceed human capabilities. If the feeling functions can also be added and housed in human form, the machine could become the man-made device that rivals natural man. The possibility becomes increasingly plausible as technology advances and as man threatens his own survival by polluting the earth. History in the distant future may be written by machines that describe how natural man was extinguished by an environment to which he was unable to adjust. While man may go the way of dinosaurs, he has a chance of passing on most of his attributes to a hardier species of his own making.

PSYCHOLOGICALLY, THE THEORY REGARDS THE HUMAN AS THE SAME AS THE RAT

Skinner has repeatedly denied that statement, but it continues to be regarded as an appropriate criticism by many people. It is a common practice, however, to think in terms of black and white and ignore the gray areas that make up most of our reliable knowledge. Skinner rejects the above assertion on simple grounds; he says that it is obviously false because anyone can see marked differences between rats and people. The gray statement that he makes, however, is that humans share *some* psychological features with lower animals.

More specifically, the Skinnerian argument says that all animals obey certain laws of behavior. All species alter their actions under the influence of reward. All animals, including man, modify their behavior or learn as a result of experienced consequences.

Skinner concedes that an adequate psychology of rats is insufficient to cover all human action. But he is silent about what kind of principle should be added to those he has developed from the study of lower animals. Perhaps the reason for his silence is a preoccupation on how much mileage he can get out of existing operant principles in dealing with human behavior. He says that the science of human behavior is still evolving. Its ultimate form may. be quite different from the present Skinnerian system. Yet Skinner seems to think that he has already developed the basic structure of a science of human behavior and that whatever additions may be made will not change its existing foundation. The matter is debatable, however, and only future developments can yield a definite answer.

The most frequent question asked of Skinner is: "Who is going to act as the master manipulator?" The questioner usually implies that Skinner sees himself as the only qualified person to assume that role. The popular impression is that there must be a master manipulator if and when the system is applied to the whole society. That misunderstanding is probably a carry-over from *Walden Two,* in which Frazer pulled the strings to get the community started in the right direction. But Skinner is not so naive as to think that the Walden Two approach can be applied to the entire American culture. A different perspective and strategy must be used.

In the first place, Skinner sees that we already have good intentions and aims. We want to eliminate war, crime, pollution, overpopulation, and other aversive aspects of life that plague us. We have been engaged in armed conflict for nearly a decade, although few if any people regard war as desirable. Our methods to reduce crime do not work effectively. We continue to pollute the environment despite the fact that on one wants to live in a world that threatens to become too toxic to sustain life. We are victims of political and commercial exploitation and we don't know what to do about it. In general, we don't need any czar of morality to tell us what aims we ought to have. Our central difficulty is the use of ineffective means for dealing with the conditions that create our major problems. In short, we desperately need better ways of handling social problems. These considerations comprise the Skinnerian perspective.

The second step is to correctly recognize the Skinnerian approach. Essentially, the approach is piecemeal. It implies that we can tackle one small segment of problems at a time by applying the techniques of operant behaviorism. The grand design is to increase gradually the scope of application. The design has nothing to do with *direct* manipulation of people, although the popular notion is quite the opposite. In fact, there is nothing in the whole psychology that advocates or describes any direct manipulation of people or of any other organisms. What is manipulated is the environment or, more specifically, certain key parts of the environment. Skinner wants to so arrange and manage the environment that the occurrence of harmful behavior is minimized and the probability of mutually helpful behavior is maximized. We do not need a dictator to tell us what values are best. But we do need a program of action that can effectively implement our aims. Skinner claims to have the essence of such a program.

Some critics of operant behaviorism work themselves into an untenable position regarding the point under discussion. On the one hand they either minimize or reject the Skinnerian claim that human behavior is a function of environmental conditions. But on the other hand they say that if operant behaviorism is put into effect it will make puppets of the people. It is difficult to see how people could lose their freedom and dignity if the environmental proposition is either false or too weak to be significant. But that kind of self-defeating argumentation is common in the critiques of operant behaviorism. It suggests that Skinnerian psychology induces fear and anger plus other negative emotions, which can be regarded as noise that overrides effective thinking.

DETERMINISM IS TREATED AS A PROVED PRINCIPLE OF UNLIMITED SCOPE

Skinner *assumes* determinism, but he does not make the error of claiming that it is a proved principle that applies to all human behavior. He is aware that he is making an assumption and sees the possibility that it may be wrong. He prefers to believe it on the basis of partial evidence. The point needs no further elaboration here. It will be examined more thoroughly in a later chapter.

SKINNER'S PHILOSOPHY OF SCIENCE IS NAIVE, OUTDATED, AND UNWORKABLE

This evaluation is usually voiced by people who take a certain philosophical stance toward the Newtonian concept of science. They assert that the social sciences cannot operate sufficiently on the traditional scientific model because of basic differences between natural and social phenomena. They also say that the Newtonian model is itself outmoded in physics and is no longer taken seriously by physicists and other natural scientists. Hence, Skinner is clinging to an archaic set of beliefs that simply cannot yield adequate outcomes.

Skinner's reply to this criticism seems to run as follows. First, we should not take too seriously philosophical prescriptions aimed at telling scientists what is good and bad in scientific affairs. The philosopher is pretty much confined to the use of logical analysis and a set of intuitive assertions, neither of which is an infallible guide in making proper assessments of a science. The analytical philosophers attempt to judge the logical consistency of scientific statements and to identify the basic criteria of meaning. Their appraisals often have little to do with the utility of scientific systems. It is perhaps impossible to adhere rigorously to standards of pure logic in developing a science, and it apparently does little good to use the philosophical criteria of meaning as guidelines. What exists in the world of empirical events cannot be legislated by logic, nor can it be expected to accord with preformed philosophical opinions. There is value in assuming a naive position toward reality. A certain humility is necessary for producing the kind of consensus that science demands.

Second, the criticisms of Newtonian physics take little account of the many practical uses of the system. Engineers who build bridges, design new devices to meet desired specifications, and deal with all sorts of other technological problems have no need to adopt Heisenberg's principle of indeterminacy. Nor is it necessary that they bother about other philosophical arguments that arise in the study of microcosmic and macrocosmic problems. Physics is a highly developed science. Psychology is a comparative infant, less mature than physics just before Newton. We are far from exploring the microcosmic and macrocosmic levels of psychological reality comparable to those explored in physics. Perhaps when we get to that stage, a Heisenberg of psychology may have something important to offer. Operant behaviorism is minimally dependent upon pure speculation. It deals primarily with the world of observable interaction between the person and his surroundings, and is not presented as the ultimate psychology. There is much value in keeping a scientific system somewhat simple in its early stages of development. Fashionable prescriptions offered by philosophers can be profitably ignored, particularly during the formative stage of a science.

Related to this criticism are those of the phenomenological psychologists, who are unhappy with Skinner because he fails to stress human intentionality and because of his effort to be purely objective. Intentionality is a fundamental part of experience, and little if any value can come from the collection and charting of data if it is ignored. Also, objectivity is an illusion because it creates a false separation within the "subject-object unity." Psychological phenomena cannot be studied effectively as isolated bits; they must be seen as belonging to integrated wholes. Skinner is too naive along these lines. He shows little grasp of the nature of human experience. Hence, his methods are totally inadequate for building a sound science of human behavior.

Skinner does not seem to be much impressed by the phenomenologists, as reflected by his debates with Rogers and by his participation in a symposium devoted to discussions on behaviorism and phenomenology. (See references at the end of the chapter.) He would maintain that despite the loopholes in his system, which are claimed by the phenomenologists to be so important, his behaviorism has proved much more practical in dealing with a wide variety of everyday problems than has any psychology based on phenomenology.

My own opinion is that, first, phenomenologists make some good criticisms of traditional methods of research. For example, in the field of survey research, where much time is given to the collection and interpretation of opinions, the data are often insufficient because they fail to reflect the perspective of the respondents. Conclusions and generalizations typically drawn are excessive, given the data collected, because they fail to reflect the full domain from which they are drawn. The artificial splintering of human perceptions that results from inducing people to respond to forced choice items can hardly serve any purpose that is significant. Surveys often lack a sufficient scope of data.

I also suspect that many psychologists who want to be labeled "phenomenological psychologists" lack a good grasp of the philosophy from which they borrow. Edmund Husserl, the acknowledged father of phenomenology, is extremely difficult to follow. His theory of essences, for example, is a most abstract doctrine that is not without equivocation. It is questionable that even professional philosophers, for the most part, grasp it as Husserl intended. So it is possible that psychologists may get in over their heads when wading into the murky depths of that philosophy. Also, Heidegger, who promoted the incorporation of phenomenology into the field of psychiatry, probably overwhelms most psychologists by his involved and abstract mode of expression. Until a reasonable consensus emerges among the phenomenological psychologists as to just what propositions are basic to their position and until they can demonstrate their claims by producing results consistent with them, it is difficult to decide about the real value of the movement.

My third impression of phenomenology is that it threatens to destroy one of the basic features of science that sets it apart from other disciplines. Science is dedicated to the discovery of reliable information that can be cast into general principles, to the development of techniques of investigation and methods of application of confirmed theorems. It is a *progressive* enterprise. And as such it must have a means of consolidating its gains, which depends somewhat on the possibility of reaching consensus about the validity of its ongoing contributions. It is necessary that qualified workers in a science be able to examine the same events and independently arrive at the same conclusions, regardless of whatever differences they may have in culture, personality traits, religion, or philosophy. In physics, chemistry, and the biological sciences, a high degree of agreement is rather common. While other features, such as correctness and utility, are important to science, methods of independent assessment resulting in consensus or near-consensus are vital to its integrity and growth. The nonsciences lack a means for producing general agreement, suggesting that consensus is not an essential aspect of them. Controversies in the arts are never settled definitively. Arguments among philosophers end without universal agreement. Theologians and mystics do not settle their differences. They simply grow tired of old problems and invent new ones, and when the new ones grow stale they often dig up old ones for reexamination. But partly *because* the nonsciences lack a means of consensus, their contributions are valuable. They are provocative and generate worthwhile problems. We owe much to the nonscientific fields. But if science is to survive it must maintain a way of repudiating false claims and hence achieving a good measure of consensus. The subjective relativism of phenomenology seems to threaten the achievement of consensus, which is so important to science. Although phenomenology is touted as the master science, it seems to have no clear-cut means for establishing consensus among investigators of different intentionalities, different values, different perspectives, and the like. It seems doubtful that the criticisms coming from the phenomenologists, pertinent as they seem, will seriously dampen the development of operant behaviorism.

A final note on phenomenology is worth consideration. It refers to the doubtful value of phenomenology when translated into a popular movement, which has the earmarks of an intellectual fad as described by Jean-François Revel. He says that intellectual fads or fashions have the following features:

1. *They have a global range.* This property helps to satisfy the need for a universal account of reality, particularly at a time when the scientific disciplines have become highly specialized and difficult to grasp by the general run of intelligent people. I would add that this need helps to keep religion viable, as both science and philosophy become more abstruse. The need for an overall, understandable explanation of reality is particularly satisfied when the believer can find an orientation that allows him to assume a significant position within the universal scheme. Popular phenomenol-

ogy provides that illusion by putting the perceiver at the center of creation. But it fails to supply the kind of solid support to the ego found in religion.

2. *Their survival is independent of their validity.* For example, the shortcomings of Marxism are widely known, and yet it survives despite the fact that much of it fails to check with hard facts.

3. *They introduce new labels that can be easily attached to all sorts of things beyond their original reference.* For example, Einstein's notion of relativity has a special meaning within his theory. But when it became fashionable to acknowledge Einstein's work, all sorts of things were tagged as relative: morals, values, truth, God, and so on. The concepts of "subject-object unity" and "intentionality" supplied by phenomenology can be related to almost anything in loose and vague ways.

4. *Their survival is somewhat independent of a strong knowledge base.* Usually only a semblance of the original concept is known, suggesting that the faddist is less interested in understanding than in creating the appearance of being hip by making it known that he is aware of the "in thing."

5. *They produce the pretension that they are superior to science; that is, they pretend to outstrip science in knowledge.* But the pretention has little foundation, because when the fashionable claim is analyzed, its substance is seen to be scarcely more than wishful thinking. It seems that many people need the comfort offered by simple explanations and that they are either unwilling to do the hard work of rigorously pursuing reliable knowledge or feel incompetent and overwhelmed. So it becomes easier to settle for a pretended wisdom, although it is unstable and vulnerable to the winds of fashion. Intellectual fads *do* provide a service.

Phenomenology is a difficult philosophy. It initially promises to be only a straightforward account of direct experience, but it quickly becomes the most abstract and abstruse web of complexity ever invented by the minds of philosophers. The mere process of making it popular virtually assures its misrepresentation. Its popularity in psychology suggests that it operates therein as a fad, having the above characteristics. Skinner's reluctance to accept phenomenology may be based on his perception of its fadlike qualities.

THEORIES OF LEARNING HAVE NO VALUE IN PSYCHOLOGY

Skinner has the reputation of being antitheory. In the early fifties he wrote a paper entitled "Are Theories of Learning Necessary?" If the paper is given only casual attention it yields the impression that Skinner is against all theories of learning. But when he used the word "theory" in that paper Skinner was referring to a special kind of learning theory which was popular among psychologists at the time. It was the kind of theory developed by Hull, who assembled a set of basic postulates or axioms, in the manner of Euclidean geometry, from which to crank out logical predictions, which were tested under laboratory conditions. Skinner's main criticism of the Hullian system was that it accepted postulates that could not be evaluated by the experiments used to test the predictions. For example, the notion that certain nerve impulses behave in a particular way cannot be verified by watching rats run through mazes. Skinner thinks that the main working propositions of a science should be based on actual data rather than merely being assumed or borrowed from another science. Speculations that cannot be evaluated by observations within the given discipline are in danger of becoming outmoded in the area from which they are borrowed. For example, psychologists sometimes borrow physiological notions while collecting facts which can neither support nor deny them. But as time passes physiology progresses, and it may discard the concepts borrowed by psychologists. So some psychological theories retain notions from other disciplines that themselves no longer accept these notions.

Skinner did not say that all learning theories are un-necessary. He simply voiced doubts about one kind of theory.

OPERANT BEHAVIORISM IS THE SAME AS
STIMULUS-RESPONSE PSYCHOLOGY

Critics who make this error of judgment are often intel-lectuals with limited knowledge of psychological systems. But their criticisms get wide publicity because of their status and their skill in writing.

Skinner's system is a special variety of behaviorism, and it differs sharply from the traditional form at certain points. The classical stimulus-response notions hold that all be-havior can be described by the stimulus-response (S-R) formula. In other words, each response is preceded by par-ticular stimuli that *elicit*—forcibly draw forth—the response. This idea implies that it is possible to search for and find stimuli and mechanisms that can account for all behavior in terms of the S-R pattern. Skinner rejects that claim, because he says that most behavior of psychological im-portance is originally *emitted* and not elicited. An emitted response is simply accepted as a fact, a given, that resists the attempt to find its stimulus cause. Emitted behavior, there-fore, suggests that the organisms is capable of *initiating* ac-tion. The S-R idea, on the other hand, suggests that the organism is passive and reacts only when aroused, and that the source of arousal can be identified.

The difference described above between the two behavior-isms is fundamental, because the S-R form conceives of human nature as unmistakably mechanistic. The term "mechanistic" refers to the science of mechanics, which deals with the motion of bodies under the influence of certain forces. In that science, any physical thing is completely controlled by the laws of motion. That is, it never initiates action; it is only a passive body pushed around by external forces. Such is the essence of mechanics. Skinner's system is deterministic, but it is also less mechanistic than classical behaviorism because it leaves room for doubt about causation, particularly about the *specific* cause of an original act. If the organism can initiate action without any identifiable stimulus source that can be isolated as such, it cannot be accepted as a part of a purely mechanistic scheme. Skinner assumes determinism, but he does not insist that it is always capable of demonstration. Thus, the margin of doubt that he entertains gives his system a less rigid status in the scientific realm than the older S-R theory.

Classical behaviorism is clearly mechanistic in that its makers seem compelled to invent mechanisms that account for such events as reinforcement. Skinner refrains from doing so. The S-R inventions are usually hypothetical mechanisms existing somewhere inside the body. Skinner readily admits the limitations of his system in terms of explanatory power, and he thinks that in so doing he escapes many knotty problems that psychology, at its present stage of development, is unable to solve.

In general, operant behaviorism is more flexible than the S-R theory, because it leaves room for future developments to fill in the gaps that at present can be bridged only by using questionable speculations. It is unlikely, therefore, that science, in its future evolution, will discard operant behaviorism as readily is it may discard the S-R system. Because Skinner's psychology is a collection of principles that are derived from observable facts and because it contains no hypothetical mechanisms for explanatory purposes, its future seems rather secure, although it is likely to undergo considerable change.

The stimulus-response psychology has had considerably less impact upon the world of practical affairs than has operant behaviorism. For example, in eduaction the S-R theory has given us significantly fewer techniques for dealing with classroom behavior than the Skinnerian system. The two perspectives differ in fundamental ways, and they entail different modes of conceptualization, experimentation, and application. It is therefore erroneous to regard them as equivalent.

The foregoing list of inadequate criticisms is only a sample, but it is reasonably representative of the kinds of reactions that occur to operant behaviorism. It is unfortunate that these and similar statements receive wide acceptance, while more substantial criticisms are seldom stressed. Let us now turn to those criticisms of operant behaviorism that have more credibility than those just covered.

DEFICIENCIES OF OPERANT BEHAVIORISM

The following criticisms are not exhaustive, but they cover the major soft spots in the system as I perceive them, and they are more substantial than the misconceptions just cited.

SKINNER'S ANALYSIS OF COMPLEX HUMAN BEHAVIOR SOMETIMES EXTENDS BEYOND THE LIMITS OF EXPERIMENTAL VERIFICATION

The spirit of operant behaviorism is to stress facts and relationships with minimal dependence upon speculative explanation. Skinner is impressed by principles that can be demonstrated and that arise from a body of experimental evidence; he finds little value in explanations that are immune to verification. He has expressed that spirit admirably in dealing with the behavior of rats and pigeons. But when it comes to certain human behaviors of a complex sort, his verbal analyses appear to go beyond the kinds of experimental tests to which he subscribes. This criticism is not just a repetition of the rejected "the rat is not the same as the human" argument. It is quite different. It holds that while Skinner may be theoretically correct in analyzing all sorts of human behavior, he reaches a point where it does not seem possible to demonstrate the validity of his verbal account by experimental means. For example, the writing of a novel involves so many unobservable activities that it does not seem possible to demonstrate experimentally all the reinforcement contingencies that are presumed to exist. Perhaps the best that Skinnerians can do in dealing with such phenomena is to come up with verbal accounts that are logically consistent with the system but may resist either rejection or support on strictly experimental grounds. In general, the realm of action that is ordinarily deemed creative and that involves imagination, thought, and speculation, behavior that is not easily open to direct observation, presents difficulties on the experimental level.

Skinner maintains that making a poem is analogous to having a baby or to the process of laying an egg by a hen. There is no creative act that is autonomous, because given a person with a particular background and living under certain conditions, whatever he "creates," such as a poem, is a function of how the environment has treated him. The poem is not some miraculous or uncaused event. That analysis is clear and is coherent within the system, and it may be correct. But it may be difficult if not impossible to demonstrate.

SKINNER'S EXPERIMENTAL MODEL HAS
LIMITED RELEVANCE

The range and significance of any theory are limited by
the assumptions and conditions under which the theory was
generated. An adequate test of the implications of a scientific system can hardly occur outside this limited sphere.
So the important question becomes: what are the legitimate
bounds of operant behaviorism? One limiting factor is the
experimental model used to generate the data that support
the concepts of the theory. The Skinnerian model of experimentation contains the following features: (1) a small and
uncomplicated environmental setting, for example, the Skinner Box; (2) unrestrained movement of the animal within
that environment; (3) a means for recording the frequency
of a chosen response; (4) control by the experimenter of the
reinforcement schedule; (5) selection of a response that has
an observable effect on some aspect of the environment;
(6) control over deprivation for a period just preceding the
experiment; (7) selection of an animal other than human.
The experiment is divided into two phases with an occasional addition of a third phase. The first phase is an
adaptation period, a time to allow the animal to get used
to the new environment. Skinner found that animals are not
ready for operant conditioning immediately after being put
into a strange setting. They are usually too excited by the
new situation and they spend time in sniffing about, investi-
gating the nooks and crannies, and so on. Some psychologists claim that this exploratory behavior is a process called
"mapping the area" and is an important prelude to later
learning. Skinner rejects such terms and simply accepts the
fact that it takes some time for a rat to cool down after
being placed in a new situation. The second phase is shaping, that is, changing the probability of a selected response
by making reward contingent upon it. For example, Skinner

decides to condition bar-pressing in a rat. So he equips the cage with a movable lever that is connected to a dispensing mechanism: each time the rat presses the bar, a pellet of food drops in a cup just below the bar. When the rat is hungry and after he has simmered down from exploring the cage, he is ripe for conditioning. Sooner or later he will step on the bar or move it with some part of his body. When that occurs, a food pellet drops and the rat immediately investigates the cup and consumes the food. The rat is apparently capable of making a connection between pressing the bar and the immediate consequence. So the probability of his again pressing the bar increases. In a relatively short time, the rat presses the bar with considerable frequency.

The third phase that is sometimes added is called the "maintenance phase." It involves a shift in the reinforcement schedule. Shaping usually occurs under continuous reinforcement, while maintenance, which strengthens a given response, occurs under one of the intermittent schedules.

Skinner has collected great quantities of data by using the model described above, and he has developed the principle of reinforcement and allied concepts therefrom. Any conditioning that occurs under the above specifications can clearly be deemed operant conditioning. But it is difficult if not impossible to fit all human learning into the operant pattern. For example, a child hears his teacher say that the moon is about 240,000 miles from the earth. He has never heard nor read that fact before, and shows no particular evidence that he has retained it until it is asked for on a test, whereupon he answers the item correctly. In this case, it is not likely that operant conditioning can be demonstrated. There is no repetition of the response. The fact was simply heard once and later given in response to a test item. Whether or not the child thought about it in the meantime or practiced saying it to himself and somehow got reinforced can only be guessed.

Why do many people retain a miscellaneous assortment of trivia? I can recall all sorts of things experienced in the distant and near past, things that occurred only once and which were quite unimportant. For example, about ten years ago I can recall a visitor from across town who said just before he left, "Well, I think that I'll go home and watch 'Route 66.' " I cannot think of any reinforcing condition that kept that trivial statement from being quickly forgotten. I can clearly remember an equally trivial remark that occurred forty-four years ago in elementary school, when a boy named Jack casually remarked that every time he crossed the street he automatically looked first to the left. And over thirty-seven years ago I accidentally overheard a girl named Ruth, who had no special attractiveness in my perspective, say that she went to bed early the night before, about ten o'clock. I don't think that any such responses had a special history of reinforcement. Skinner says that forgetting occurs as a function of time. A response simply fades away unless given occasional reinforcement. If that is true, I should have long ago been relieved of a useless assortment of trivia. I don't think that I am unique in holding the dubious distinction of remembering such things. I suspect that nearly all adults share the same distinction. I see no way of demonstrating by means of the operant system how such responses resist forgetting.

It is also difficult to use the Skinnerian model to condition thinking and other covert responses, because covert behavior is outside the realm of observation. Since an observable response and an observable consequence are conditions central to operant conditioning, the whole area of covert behavior can be handled only by speculation, which is not most compatible with the Skinnerian spirit.

Another important example is reading. Although Skinnerian methods have been used to teach reading, the operant system is not easily used to account for learning via reading *after* the skill has been learned. More specifically, a person reads an item in the daily paper. It has no special appeal to him. But a week later, during a conversation, he repeats the essence of the item. Skinner would say that the latter situation contained certain stimuli that shared properties with those present during the original reading. But that is pure speculation and may be imposible to show. Acquiring new information from reading does not seem to fit the Skinnerian model.

SKINNER'S ANALYSIS OF PUNISHMENT APPEARS, AT BEST, ONLY PARTIALLY TRUE

Punishment may not be as bad as Skinner asserts. There seems to be increasing evidence that a combination of threat and reinforcement is more effective in learning than reinforcement alone. A rat put into a Y-maze learns to run to the left more quickly if he gets a mild shock when he runs to the right and gets a pellet of food when he runs to the left than if only the reward is used.

The natural, nonsocial environment contains both aversive and positive stimuli. The stresses imposed by threats may be necessary to the evolutionary process. If not for the existence of noxious conditions it is possible that vegetation would be the only life form existent. The need for locomotion and means of manipulation would hardly arise if the natural environment contained only benign conditions for living things. Without stresses and threats, it is hard to conceive of the growth of adaptive processes. Freud thought adjustment to stress was the key to human development, although he was quite aware of the dangers of excessive stress.

The Skinnerian design for a new society seems to contain special means for eliminating stress in the forms of threat and punishment. While his intent may be heartily approved by most people, he does not have sufficient evidence to show just what would happen in a complex system devoid of man-made threats and punishment. It would seem that the psychology of punishment is more complicated than Skinner thinks and that designs for social improvement may require some use of aversive stimulation. While I agree with Skinner that we now depend excessively upon threat and punishment to regulate behavior, it does not follow that its elimination would be desirable. We need further examination of the subtle qualities and effects of punishment before we can make any sweeping prescription as to its proper role.

SKINNER RECOGNIZES THE NEED FOR EXTENDING HIS SYSTEM TO INCLUDE PRINCIPLES UNIQUE TO HUMANS, BUT SO FAR HE HAS FAILED TO IDENTIFY THEM

Skinner exhibits ambivalence on this point. He admits that the science of human behavior is not complete, that it needs further development. He also admits that rats and pigeons are not perfect models of humans. It would appear, therefore, that we need some psychological principles in addition to those developed from animal data. Yet Skinner also seems to think that the foundation of a science of human behavior has been set and that only minor alterations are necessary in order to deal adequately with human behavior. But if the foregoing criticisms are reasonably valid, the system may need considerable modification before it is applicable to the full range of human behavior.

STRONG POINTS
OF OPERANT BEHAVIORISM

I have already given recognition to some of the advantages of Skinnerian psychology. Consequently, I shall not dwell on the matter in much further detail. The following outline of the virtues of the system is sufficient to acknowledge some of the important strengths of the psychology.

THE BASIC PRINCIPLES ARE FIRMLY ROOTED IN HARD FACTS

No other psychological theory has surpassed operant behaviorism in this virtue. It is a strength which resists arguments to the contrary. Judged from this point alone, the system promises to have a long survival.

THE PRINCIPLES ARE RELEVANT TO MUCH OF HUMAN BEHAVIOR, PARTICULARLY TO CONCRETE, OBSERVABLE ACTION

A great amount of everyday behavior consists of a vast network of habits. It is hard to exaggerate the importance of personal habits, because they pretty much determine the difference between effective and ineffective life styles. Probably no other psychology has provided as many techniques for dealing with habits in a practical way as has operant behaviorism. Social morality, for example, is a repertory of action according with the contingencies of reinforcement and punishment controlled by the society. A number of analysts of social organization seem to be convinced that we are experiencing a moral crisis and that the welfare of future generations depends somewhat on how we meet this crisis.

While Skinnerian psychology is commonly regarded as lacking in those values necessary for developing a workable moral system, it does promise to supply useful means for establishing those habits that are deemed to make up moral conduct. Such habits need to be reasonably homogeneous across individuals and they must be particularly strong—resistant to extinction—before they can provide the cement that protects the integrity of society. No other psychology seems to offer more promise in helping us establish a strong and viable moral code. In fact, the utility of the operant system seems to reside much more in moral training than in cognitive learning, although the two cannot be clearly separated. It would be indeed unfortunate if the weaknesses of this psychology were used as reasons to prevent its application to the urgent problems of moral training.

OPERANT BEHAVIORISM PROVIDES USEFUL CRITERIA FOR APPRAISING THE PRACTICAL VALUE OF OTHER PSYCHOLOGIES

Some of Skinner's most outstanding contributions lie in his trenchant and productive criticisms of other systems. These are often overlooked by those who evaluate his work. It is difficult to estimate their impact upon developments in modern psychology. But Skinner does have a set of standards and tools for stripping the verbal fat from psychologies that appear valid on the surface, but which turn out to be hardly more than statements of intent rather than sturdy principles of proven utility.

THE SYSTEM IS NOT CLUTTERED WITH UNNECESSARY CONCEPTS

This virtue is closely linked with the preceding one. It bears special mention because one of the main difficulties in putting many psychologies to practical use lies in their esoteric jargon, which can be interpreted in almost any way that the reader desires. This is particularly true of a number of theories of human personality. The Skinnerian system is especially strong in providing principles that can be readily understood if one does not succumb to the emotional turbulence that the ideas tend to arouse. In fact, Skinner's own description of his psychology is so lean and free from verbal noise that its very austerity may actually cause his readers some problems. I have tried to adopt a less parsimonious form of exposition than Skinner's in the hope that it will make the reader feel more at home in his effort to learn.

While some advantages of operant psychology may have been omitted in this brief outline, I believe that enough has been said about its strengths to convince the reader that it is a mistake to yield to the impulse of rejecting it totally simply because it contains some significant shortcomings. Perhaps no other system has more to offer those who work in practical fields wherein psychological problems abound. Yet one can also err by accepting it uncritically and particularly by trying to apply it in a mechnical and unthoughtful way. As is true of all other major psychologies, it has both strong and weak points. The reader should apprise himself of both aspects before he makes any final assessment.

FOR FURTHER READING

SKINNER, B. F. *Science and Human Behavior*. New York: Macmillan Company, 1953.

———. *Walden Two*. New York: Macmillan Company, 1948.

WANN, T. W. ed. *Behaviorism and Phenomenology: Constrasting Bases for Modern Psychology.* Chicago: University of Chicago Press, 1964.

REVEL, JEAN-FRANÇOIS. "Intellectual Fashions," *The Center Magazine,* January/February 1973.

part Two

PROBLEMS
OF FREEDOM

CHAPTER 3

Meanings of Freedom

A FOUR-PART CLASSIFICATION

Freedom has many meanings. Some meanings are concrete while others are abstract. It is difficult to make an exhaustive list of the definitions that have been assigned to freedom. Any successful attempt to do so would require a separate book, particularly if each definition were given adequate treatment. A glossary of that sort is fortunately not necessary to my present aims. It is important, however, to get a good sample of the meanings that have been imposed on the word "freedom." I have selected thirteen statements which I think capture the major notions, and present them below with a brevity that I hope will not curtail clarity.

1. Freedom is the exercise of choice without coercion.
2. It is doing whatever one wants to do regardless of consequence.

3. It is a feeling that arises from recognition of self-control.

4. It is the absence of determinism.

5. It is an existential condition of a person who realizes his true uniqueness and essential loneliness.

6. Freedom is the act of avoidance of or escape from aversive situations.

7. It is something necessarily implied by the fact that human behavior cannot be fully predicted.

8. It is the degree of latitude that one can exercise within the structure of natural and social laws.

9. Freedom is a product of learning; that is, the more knowledge one has that he can use effectively the more freedom he has. For example, the illiterate person lacks the freedom to perform some acts that the literate person can perform.

10. Freedom is the ability to express dissent no matter how strong the coercion to do otherwise.

11. Freedom is a derivative of power. The more power one has the greater his freedom, because as one's power increases the more personal desires he can translate into action.

12. It is essentially a mode of awareness or state of mind. It is one of the natural ways that we interpret personal experience.

13. Freedom exists only as a conscious assumption that one makes about himself in relation to his aspirations within some context. The assumption is that one *can* carry out his own feasible plans if he so desires.

These thirteen meanings obviously overlap. They can be sorted by means of a variety of classification systems. For example, one simple system is a twofold sorting: absolute versus relative freedom. Another dichotomy is innate and acquired freedoms. But a functional sorting probably requires more categories than two. I have created a taxonomy of four classes as a springboard for further analysis. The purpose of that analysis is to identify the basic conceptions of freedom and to examine the grounds on which each is based. If the analysis is reasonably successful it should help clarify the nature of substance of the various propositions on which our notions of freedom seem to rest. Skinner claims that much of the popular belief in freedom is fictitious and therefore provides dubious grounds for taking action, particularly efforts to solve our main social problems. Our analysis should help to examine the tenability of Skinner's claim, to pinpoint its possible strengths and weaknesses. Also, it should furnish some working criteria with which to assess the various criticisms that have been leveled against the Skinnerian thesis about freedom. And lastly, the analysis should be helpful in later efforts to identify the substance of academic freedom and other notions of freedom found in education.

I shall first condense the above statements of freedom and number each one for ready reference.

1. Choice without coercion.
2. Doing as one desires—acting on impulse.
3. Feeling of self-control.
4. Absence of determinism.
5. Property of existential self.
6. Avoidance or escape.
7. Margin of unpredictability of human behavior.
8. Latitude within laws.
9. Function of learning—use of knowledge.
10. Expression of dissent.
11. Function of power.
12. Mode of perception.
13. Conscious assumption that one *can* implement plans.

These thirteen meanings can be sorted into four major classes:

(a) Self-autonomy: this property is implied by statements 1, 2, 3, 5, 10, and 13.

(b) Indeterminacy inherent in the universe: implied by numbers 4, 7, and 8.

(c) Human growth function: implied by 6, 9, and 11.

(d) Basic trait of human cognition: implied by statement 12.

FREEDOM AND DETERMINISM

It is obvious that the above sorting is not completely satisfactory, because the four classes are not sufficiently independent. One can argue, for example, that class (b) is the most general one and can include the other three. The most basic consideration therefore, is whether or not a principle of indeterminacy pervades all reality. The most cogent arguments bearing on this point are made by physicists, who disagree about Heisenberg's principle of uncertainty. If the universe is composed of events that cannot be described deterministically, no matter how adequate the means of observation, some principle of uncertainty must be accepted. Let us examine briefly the pro and con arguments on this issue to see what validity can be assigned to the claim of indeterminism. Since I am not a physicist I must rely on the analysis of others who are better qualified. The following treatment is borrowed from various sources, particularly from the book *Determinism and Freedom in the Age of Modern Science*, a collection of over twenty-five articles representing the proceedings of the first annual New York University Institute of Philosophy. Bridgman and other scientists plus an array of philosophers contributed articles to the proceedings which were edited by Sidney Hook.

Among classical physicists determinism was apparently unquestioned. They thought it was theoretically possible to predict the path of any particle during its entire future if its velocity and position were known along with other forces that impinge upon it. But in quantum mechanics the future path of a subatomic particle cannot be predicted, because its position and velocity cannot both be known at once. The greater the accuracy in measuring the position of a particle the greater the error in the measurement of its velocity, and vice versa; accuracy in the measurement of one parameter is negatively correlated with accuracy in measurement of the other. Heisenberg expressed this relationship mathematically in a statement of inequality.

The reason that both position and velocity cannot be determined simultaneously is that any system used to observe the particle interacts with the particle. More specifically, there is an interchange of energy between the observing system and the object. Hence, the very act of observation alters the behavior of the particle. No clear-cut distinction can be made between the particle and the observing system because of the energy exchange between the two; their boundaries apparently fuse in some zone of interaction. This nebulous fusion means that the particle cannot be identified independent of the system of observation. It becomes a part of a larger whole.

There is no argument about the experimental facts. But there is considerable controversy about their interpretation. The determinists say that the principle of uncertainty refers only to experimental imperfection, which implies nothing about the lack of causation in nature. Uncertainty, according to them, is inherent in methods of observation and measurement and not in nature.

Bohr and perhaps most other psysicists disagree with the deterministic interpretation. They say that because the future position of a particle cannot be accurately predicted, we have no evidence to say that both position and velocity actually exist for the particle at a given instant. Scientists cannot afford to assert as factual any claim that cannot be supported by evidence. If there is no possible way to determine position and velocity at the same instant, we have no grounds for actually believing that they both exist as simultaneous phenomena. Therefore, it is more sensible to accept uncertainty than to adhere rigidly to determinism; the evidence does not and cannot support determinism.

If there is no way to make a clear separation between the object and the system of observation, we cannot speak clearly about the object per se. We must speak about an interaction system instead, and we must alter our whole conceptual scheme about the domain of data. When an "object" is observed, the data produced are not simply facts about the object alone; they are reports of a system of events that extends beyond any clear-cut boundaries of the object. It is not possible to limit data only to the behavior of the object. Since the final court of appeal in settling any scientific dispute lies in the data, the case for determinism, at the microcosmic level, may forever remain unsupported.

Even the predictive validity of statistical procedures in dealing with the distribution of subatomic particles cannot rescue determinism because of the basic disputes about the meaning of probability.

According to Bridgman, the argument by Bohr was an effort to support the idea that any event is only a part of a larger whole, to uphold the belief that no new methods can be discovered to reinstate determinism, and to construct a logical means of thinking about the facts. Perhaps the most questionable part of Bohr's position is the belief that future technology will not create any means of observation that can eliminate the energy interchange between the object and the system of observation. This is a prediction about what *cannot* be done.

In his book *Profiles of the Future,* Clarke gives several examples to show how vulnerable experts can be when they predict what is impossible in science. He states "Clarke's Law": "When a distinguished but elderly scientist states that something is possible, he is almost certainly right. When he states that something is impossible, he is very probably wrong." Clarke defines an elderly scientist as one over thirty. When this "law" is applied to Bohr's prediction about future means of observation, the edge in the debate swings back to the determinists.

The determinists assume that the subatomic particle is an object and therefore exists in time as a continuity of physical properties and behaves according to certain laws. Bohr and his protagonists make a similar assumption, except they see the particle (object) as a part of a larger whole, independent of which it cannot be fully described. But suppose both assumptions are incorrect. Suppose the subatomic particle cannot be considered as an object or even as a physical entity in a subject-object whole. Let us assume that it is only a quality in a matrix of physical events, and that it has *neither* velocity nor position. When we set up an experiment to determine velocity, the velocity is not something that can be assigned to the particle, but is nothing more than a product of the situation that we produce and has no inherent attachment to a quantum. Hence the principle of uncertainty does not apply to any tiny thing but only to an experimental arrangement. The upshot of this twist is that the principle of uncertainty carries no threat to determinism. It seems likely that assumptions other than the proposed one could be identified, resulting in removal of the controversy. Therefore, the issue between the determinists and those who hold to the principle of uncertainty rests on an assumption set, and it is possible to substitute other assumptions that may remove the strong differences of interpretation.

We should also keep in mind another point that Bridgman makes to explain why physicists disagree so sharply on the matter. He says that more than science is involved. He sees emotion, habits of thought, and religion coming into the picture. "The Lord God does not throw dice," said Einstein.

Because the problem extends beyond existing science, the issue is basically philosophical.

The net result of the argument is that no solid ground exists to accept or discard determinism with any degree of finality. The issue is unsettled. Therefore, the most fundamental category of freedom in our taxonomy has no compelling support.

Arguments both for and against self-autonomy, the first element in the taxonomy, are found to be more speculative than is indeterminacy in physics. Those who believe that autonomy is a property of the self or the mind do so largely on intuitive grounds. While they cite some favorable evidence, they do not come up with the clincher, namely, to show that choice, itself, is undetermined by outer events. But the determinists have an equally questionable position because they cannot describe the process of decision making in objective terms with a satisfactory degree of completeness. Something is going on inside the person, and whether that something is a purely deterministic process is a matter more of conjecture than of certainty. Again, the argument ends up in the same kind of stalemate. Both positions are about equally plausible and about equally doubtful.

When freedom is defined as a human growth function it is usually associated with learning and with certain kinds of maturation. There are at least two schools of thought that relate to this kind of freedom: one is deterministic and the other is based on self-autonomy. We have already seen that autonomy is an assumption, not a concrete fact. Therefore, let us look at the deterministic idea of freedom as it relates to learning. On common-sense grounds the term "deterministic freedom" seems to make little sense, because the two words are not compatible. But with a little explanation, the idea can take on a meaning that does not insult our intelligence. In the first place, we can think of freedom as any act that allows the person to surmount obstacles or that permits him to escape from or avoid unpleasant situations. For example, a person driving a car has a flat tire. His freedom to continue driving in a normal way is interrupted by the flat, which serves as a barrier or obstacle. So he stops to exchange the flat for his good spare tire. He then proceeds on his way *free from* the impediment. He has removed the barrier and has thereby gained a measure of freedom. Nearly all problem solving is a freedom-making process.

In order to gain freedom, in the above sense, the person must learn certain skills and apply them appropriately. For example, the skilled golfer is able to avoid most of the problems that plague the duffer. And when he makes a bad shot he can usually overcome his momentary disadvantage more effectively than can the unskilled player. Hence, the skilled person—one who has learned well—is *freer* to carry out his intentions successfully than one who has failed to acquire a comparable level of achievement. Determinism now comes into the picture by conceiving of learning in a deterministic fashion. If freedom depends upon learning, and if learning is itself determined, then freedom is not autonomous. The behaviorists, including Skinner, describe the learning process along deterministic lines. But the main weakness of the behavioristic position is that *some* kinds of learning cannot fit neatly into such a scheme. Creative thinking is a case in point. Problem solving that requires the integration of concepts so as to form general principles, such as was developed by Newton in the field of mechanics, cannot be fully attributed to outer causes. Newton know about certain facts as discovered by Galileo and others. But he also had to manipulate those facts symbolically and bring them together in a coherent pattern before his laws of motion could be explicitly stated. No one seems to know just what happens on the higher levels of problem solving, although many conjectures based on determinism have been offered. But we are sure that such problem solving occurs. Since the deterministic explanation becomes progressively weaker—i.e., relies increasingly on supposition—as learning becomes more complex and more abstract, it cannot claim absolute superiority over autonomy at those levels. Hence the argument between the two camps again ends in a deadlock. The nature of that deadlock is testimony to the vast area of ignorance still prevalent about learning, freedom, personality, and kindred topics. Such ignorance suggests that the most sensible attitude toward the deterministic-freedom issue is one of uncertainty. Both arguments have serious weaknesses. They compel us to conclude that freedom and determinism are essentially areas of speculation; they are convenient and often useful ideas for dealing with reality. They can also be deceptive.

The fourth major meaning of freedom is the notion that the human is wired neurologically so as to interpret some experience as autonomous. In other words, the way a person is put together biologically predisposes him to use freedom as one category of perception. The claim implies that the freedom concept contributes to survival. If we regarded ourselves only as passive pawns we would have little inclination to cope. So it is useful to assume that we can initiate action, that we can deliberately have some impact on the world about us. We are not purely dependent upon circumstances. In fact, we need some measure of independence. But more accurately, we need to *regard* ourselves as at least partially free. Nature provides the freedom mode of perception as a vehicle for survival. In addition, this position says that our perception of reality is not a valid picture of existence because what is real to us can be only our impression of existence. True existence cannot be experienced in its pure state. Therefore, we cannot *know* whether it operates in a causal way or not. And what we experience is colored by how we are put together, by our structure. It is idle to make absolute claims about the exact nature of existence. We can only perceive within the limits of our natural make-up. But part of that make-up is a faith in and need for a measure of freedom. Nature gives us the capacity to cope, and when we develop that capacity we ipso facto regard ourselves as having a degree of freedom. Again, freedom has no independent and absolute existence. Rather, it is a quality of human perception, a way that we see ourselves in relation to other things.

This position is stated in such a way that it is probably impossible to test. It can be an attractive haven for those who have become weary of wrestling with the problem of freedom and with other equally baffling concepts. It is a "solution" that rests purely upon speculation and hence carries no threat to the above conclusion, namely, that both freedom and determinism are convenient hypotheses that can be both useful and dysfunctional.

Skinner says that freedom is concretely manifested in avoidance of and escape from aversive conditions. But before such freedom can have much scope, the person must build up a good repertory of behavior, which is acquired principally by the operation of reinforcement contingencies. Thus, Skinner's notion of freedom can be cast in the framework of determinism. Since the building of a behavior repertory is determined by environmental conditions, freedom depends upon the conditions to which one responds.

There is both strength and weakness in Skinner's definition. Its weakness is its limited scope, its confining of freedom to avoidance and escape. Its strength lies in its concreteness and its utility as a scientific concept. It is demonstrably functional and it carries much of the practical meaning that is assigned to freedom. It tends to antagonize many people because it rules out personal autonomy, which not only seems self-evident but which is commonly held in high esteem as well. A more detailed account of the limitations that Skinnerian freedom contains will be given in a later chapter.

Skinner, of course, is not the only psychologist who sees freedom as a growth function. Other learning theorists imply that the accumulation of knowledge and skills equips the person to increase his range of alternatives so that freedom of choice can be exercised. Learning a skill such as reading or writing increases personal freedom because one can select freely, for example, among a variety of reading materials. A library does not increase the freedom of the illiterate person, because he can perform no meaningful interaction with printed material, but the literate person is free to choose whatever stimulates his interest. He can discriminate between books that are exciting and dull. He can become better informed and thus increase his freedom of choice in other matters. One may learn, for example, how to repair electrical appliances by studying books and hence have the freedom to choose whether to repair a given appliance or pay for that service.

This view of freedom implies that education is or should be a major means to freedom. Also, the developmental idea is compatible with the notion that freedom is a derivative of power, *if* increase of power is a function of one's own efforts and maturation. But power may be inherited, as with, for example, economic power or, in some parts of the world, political power. If power is taken as a requisite for freedom, an equitable distribution of freedom depends upon an equitable distribution of power. But some forms of power may not be amenable to controlled distribution—for example, powers that are assumed to be genetically linked, such as physical strength.

The developmental idea of freedom hits a snag when the concept of free choice is added. Learning can amount to an accumulation of knoweldge and skills that multiply the alternatives open to one. But to think that a free choice occurs because the alternatives are available is to introduce a questionable assumption. If, as some psychologists assert, all behavior, including choice, is motivated, and most motives are unconscious, then choice is apparently determined by something over which the conscious self has little or no control. Of course, this causal hypothesis seems no more plausible than the assumption of autonomy; neither one has been conclusively confirmed. Hence, both autonomy and behavioral causality appear to be nothing more than assumptions.

CONCLUSIONS

All the definitions of freedom in the list of thirteen are based on propositions that are uncertain. But belief in complete determinism seems to have an equally hypothetical base. This leaves us with the conclusion that both freedom and determinism amount to domains of speculation. Yet it should not be concluded that cogent arguments and analysis of the problem are a waste of time. For one thing, the analysis so far suggests that whatever assumption one favors, he should have an attitude of tolerance toward the other. It does not seem profitable to be rigid either way. That the two assumptions are about equally convincing and seem to have continuing viability makes it worthwhile to explore the practical value of each one.

TOWARD A PRAGMATIC RAPPROCHEMENT

Bridgman, in his article "Determinism and Punishment," takes the position that there are two levels of experience: the free-will level and the deterministic level. He says that operations that make up daily life and social interaction require the assumption of free will because in this domain we are dealing with many events that we can neither control nor predict. One does not know just what he will be doing next month, next week, tomorrow, or even in the next ten minutes. Also, one's daily associates do all sorts of things that cannot be accurately predicted. So when we operate in such a realm it is useful to assume the free-will proposition, simply because strict determinism cannot operate. On the other hand, a deterministic frame of reference is necessary at another level of experience, principally that of scientific activity. Bridgman sees determinism as a program for directing inquiry, applicable to most of the phenomena that we experience.

Although Bridgman does not cite specific examples to show exactly where determinism is the more practical assumption and where free will is the more useful, his message is quite clear. His main point is that many situations occur in which prediction and control break down, rendering inoperative the use of determinism. Even in science the deterministic approach cannot always be successful, as shown by the Heisenberg principle. The following example and supporting statements should help to illustrate in concrete terms why determinism is not always feasible in the science of psychology.

If a person sits down to write a letter, it does not seem appropriate to assume that his writing is programmed and he simply acts as the instrument in carrying out the program. Rather, one assumes that he is faced with a large array of alternatives in the form of letters, words, modes of expression, and meanings. He must perform the task of selecting, connecting, and writing a series of symbols that correspond to certain thoughts that he fashions from the kaleidoscope of impressions which flow through his awareness. He must take some initiative in selecting items from the storehouse of available material. He may write the letter and fail to please himself, discard his effort and try again. It is so difficult to describe this complicated action by a deterministic paradigm that it seems far simpler and more appropriate to shift to the level of freedom. This does not necessarily mean that writing a letter or creating a design may not ultimately be described by deterministic theory. The important point is that the application of determinism in such areas of behavior as creating, designing, inventing, and the like is prohibitive. Even if these kinds of behavior are basically deterministic, our knowledge of how to describe them in that vein is so primitive and incomplete that our best efforts at this time are inadequate. It is much simpler and more useful to assume that free choice is operating than to wrestle with the intricacies of determinism.

Skinner says that the environment does the selecting; certain conditions in the environment predispose certain actions by the person. And what one repeats is a function of the environmental feedback given on previous occasions of the same or a similar nature. This hypothesis cannot be taken lightly, because it does seem to square with many observed facts. At least, the data do not deny the hypothesis even when the situation is too complicated to identify the specific variables. But the difficulty in testing the hypothesis with regard to behavoirs that are labeled "designing," "planning," and the like seems at this time to be overwhelming.

Perhaps the central question is: what do we mean by choosing? In everyday language, choosing implies a degree of latitude afforded by circumstances. If Skinner is correct in saying that the environment does the selecting and not the person, how does he account for behavior that occurs when the environment is ambiguous in its demand? "Ambiguous demand by the environment" is intended to refer here only to the simple fact that the environment often provides some latitude about just what pattern of behavior is to be reinforced; within this zone of latitude the person finds the condition that is termed "choice." Just what he will select in this range of freedom may be difficult if not impossible to connect with his prior history. Skinner treats this under the concept "operant behavior," which comprehends at least two things: (a) the fact that no prior stimulus can be found that triggers the response, and (b) the fact that this class of behavior imposes some energy change on the environment; that is, it acts or operates on the environment. So even in Skinner's system there is a zone of indeterminacy: the initiation of an operant response defies a causal description or actual demonstration of its determination. To say either that there exists a cause which is too camouflaged to identify or that the response is self-initiated amounts to tenuous but equally plausible speculation; there seems to be no compelling evidence to choose either pronouncement. Skinner chooses determinism because it is compatible with deterministic aspects of other parts of behavior that he is able to demonstrate. This consistency on the part of Skinner is quite understandable and defensible. More accurately, however, Skinner elects to ignore the origin of the operant response and does not bother to account for it. He says that it is roughly equivalent to "voluntary" behavior, but he makes the reservation that it is perhaps incorrect to assume identity between the operant and what is normally called a "voluntary response." So the implication is that the original operant may be determined but it is impossible to identify its antecedents. We are left, therefore, with a measure of uncertainty. It is possible to plug into operant psychology the notion of free choice and thus modify it so that it contains the kind of ambiguity that may be needed in order for a theory to survive.

Attribution of freedom is sometimes assumed to imply ignorance; that is, we use the notion only when we lack sufficient knowledge of reality to demonstrate causality. But to so assume causality is just as speculative as to invoke free choice. If the dilemma found in quantum mechanics has its counterpart in psychology, there may be no possible way to resolve the freedom-determinism issue in the area of human behavior. Perhaps the best position to hold is to make room for both assumptions and judge the validity of each position on the basis of the consequences that emerge from it.

Let us examine a few brief instances that point up the usefulness of determinism. From telltale marks of mud on the floor and the observation that a child has mud on his shoes it does not require direct observation to conclude that the child made the tracks. Puddles of water and wet ground observed in the morning can best be interpreted as caused by rain, even though the observer did not actually see the rain. Given tracks in snow that correspond to known bear tracks, it does not require observation of the animal to be rather sure that a bear traveled over the ground. A cook places a meat dish in an oven at a certain heat level under the assumption that after a certain time the meat will be done as desired; it would be irrational to assume that cooking is independent of or free from the impact of heat. All sorts of interpretations in everyday life depend upon using the deterministic assumption. The very foundation of what we call "meaning" is probably, in part, made up of the deterministic assumption. If all observed events occurred randomly, so that it was impossible to make causal interpretations, it is unlikely that human experience could have the quality that we call meaningful.

While it is convenient to assume freedom in making sense out of creative acts, it is likewise convenient and perhaps necessary to assume determinism in situations where it appears obvious that a sequence of events has occurred in which the earlier events are essential antecedents for the occurrence of later ones. Perhaps the most important conclusion is that while freedom and determinism seem logically incompatible, they are both necessary for dealing successfully with the broad spectrum of tasks in our daily lives.

SUMMARY

The various definitions of freedom can be sorted into a few classes of basic meanings, each of which rests on some proposition. "Self-autonomy" is based on the notion that there exists in each person a means for generating motivation that is relatively independent of external determiners. Although this idea appears to be self-evident or an immediately given phenomenon, not requiring further support, it conflicts with much evidence. Determinism seems to be an essential assumption for making any sense out of a wide range of experience. It is tempting to assume that attribution of self-autonomy is simply a reflection of ignorance of the determiners, but that assumption has no particular advantage. The pragmatic "solution" of the freedom-determinism issue holds that the problem has no unique answer; that is, it is untenable to assert that all behavior is autonomous and it is equally so to assume that determinism is capable of complete demonstration.

The idea that indeterminacy is an inherent property of nature, including all matter, creates an issue that so far has no satisfactory resolution. So at this most basic level, both determinacy and indeterminacy seem to be about equally compelling and equally dubious.

The argument that freedom is a human growth function, a by-product of either learning or power, both of which are somehow acquired, is also a matter of knotty equivocation. The argument, when put in a practical context, implies free choice, because as one increases his options through learning, it is expected that he can choose from among the available alternatives. But if one's acceptance or rejection of a given option is based on the consequences that are believed to ensue, both freedom and determinism enter the picture. On the one hand, the determinists can say that one's choice is determined by the perceived consequences. On the other hand, it seems equally convincing to say that the choice is made without any causal antecedents and that when one projects logically into the future to estimate consequences, he is exercising freedom and not following a pattern that can be predicted with scientific accuracy. Hence, the same set of events can be interpreted either way, and it is perhaps not tenable to claim that one interpretation is valid and the other false. This is an important aspect of the freedom issue, because it brings into the open the fact that one's viewpoint or mental set can hardly be ignored, which is why the problem has no unique answer. If that is true, we may have to accept a subjective element called "perception" and recognize that it is a factor that changes from one person to the next. We may tentatively conclude, therefore, that some people have a tendency, acquired or otherwise, to favor the deterministic mental set while others are predisposed to take the freedom frame of reference.

If freedom is taken to mean acting on impulse rather than on deliberation, the door is left open for all sorts of unconscious forces that may give rise to impulse. No one has shown that impulse is deliberately self-generated and is a product of free choice. The main difficulty in using impulse as the basis of freedom is that it can lead to consequences that are enslaving; it has dubious value for the person and for his social environment. To value as a kind of freedom a force that dissipates independence and leads to unwanted constraints appears to be unworthy of serious consideration.

The idea that freedom is a mode of cognition, turns out to be an assumption that is incapable of being confirmed or denied by hard facts. The person is alleged to be wired neurologically so that certain experiences, such as choosing, forming a new idea, or imagining, are perceived as relatively independent of external causes. Yet those same experiences can be conceived of deterministically. No crucial set of experiments has verified the validity of either position.

The upshot of all these considerations is that nature tends

to deny general preconceptions imposed upon it. To say that all the events that compose the universe are determined seems to be beyond human ability to verify. The same holds for the comparable assertion about freedom. When saddled with ignorance, which may never be reduced to zero, it seems best to fall back on some kind of pragmatic form of analysis. But the existence of the free will-deterministic problem, despite its apparently insolvable nature, is most worthy of consideration because of the insights that arise in trying to comprehend and solve it. I agree with William James:

A common opinion prevails that the juice has ages ago been pressed out of the free-will controversy, and that no new champion can do more than warm up stale arguments which everyone has heard. This is a radical mistake. I know of no subject less worn out, or in which inventive genius has a better chance of breaking open new ground—not, perhaps, or forcing a conclusion or coercing assent, but of deepening our sense of what the issue between the two parties really is, of what the ideas of fate and of free-will imply.

FOR FURTHER READING

BRIDGMAN, PERCY W. "Determinism and Punishment" and "Determinism in Modern Science," in *Determinism and Freedom in the Age of Modern Science*. Edited by Sidney Hook. New York: New York University Press, 1958.

CLARKE, ARTHUR C. *Profiles of the Future*. New York: Bantam Books, n.d.

HOOK, SIDNEY. "Necessity, Indeterminism, and Sentimentalism," in *Determinism and Freedom in the Age of Modern Science*. Edited by Sidney Hook. New York: New York University Press, 1958.

CHAPTER 4

Skinnerian Freedom: Pros and Cons

As noted before, Skinner reduces freedom to two clear-cut forms of action, namely, *escape* and *avoidance*. When a person does something to escape a harmful or unpleasant situation he is performing an act of freedom; he is ridding himself of something that is aversive. Examples are easy to cite. A person who has a headache takes a couple of aspirin tablets and gets rid of the pain. His act of taking the aspirin is instrumental in freeing himself from the pain. A person in a hot, stuffy room opens a window to let in cool air. A man attends a public lecture and finds the speaker boring. He gets up and leaves the room, freeing himself from the tiresome speech. A secretary has a boss who continually criticizes her work; she quietly finds another job and quits her old one. A nation revolts against oppressive leadership to free itself from the hardships imposed by its leaders. All of these examples illustrate the escape form of freedom.

Avoidance behavior amounts to doing something to *pre-*

vent contact with an undesirable stimulus. A child looks down the road and sees the local bully at a distance. He runs to school to get within the protection of the teacher, thus avoiding unpleasant interaction with the bully. A man gets a thorough medical checkup every year to avoid serious advancement of disease. A city council makes decisions to avoid the development of a ghetto. A nation engages in a treaty to avoid armed conflict. In general, avoidance is a class of behavior that serves to *maintain* freedom, while escape behavior *produces* freedom.

The big controversy raised by operant behaviorism is not about the existence of freedom. The argument is about the *meaning* of freedom, and it centers on such questions as the following: Is the person autonomous; that is, can he act independently of outside influences? What is the nature of choice? Is the person a helpless pawn among environmental forces? Can a full account of human behavior be cast within deterministic principles?

Skinner's answers to these questions are based on an explicit assumption, namely, that human behavior is determined or controlled by the environment. He thinks that available evidence constitutes solid ground for accepting this assumption, and that, as new research data are reported, the assumption becomes stronger. Hence there is no reason to think that future evidence will somehow reverse this trend.

Those who argue against Skinner generally agree that behavior is *partly* determined. But they strongly disagree with his prediction that all behavior will eventually be interpretable within a set of deterministic principles. Also, his opponents place much value on such notions as *choice, creativity, self-control, uniqueness of the person, spontaneity,* and *self-actualization.* These terms carry meanings and implications that are incompatible with complete determinism.

Skinnerian freedom is compatible with determinism. The tendency to escape and avoid noxious conditions is built into the genes; it is a part of the evolutionary heritage. Those individuals who could not successfully avoid or escape dangerous conditions were weeded out, while those who were most adroit in such behavior survived to procreate their own kind. Freedom has genetic roots and can be seen as part of the deterministic scheme.

The main problem is how to make an adequate evaluation of the Skinnerian thesis. Reactions to the thesis appearing in the popular press and on television and radio have failed to meet Skinner's challenge effectively. My attempt to assess it takes up a part of this book. Before the evaluation can take form, it is appropriate to look at the objections Skinner has raised to the popular beliefs on freedom.

POPULAR NOTIONS OF FREEDOM— SKINNER'S CRITICISM

Are most of the popular notions about freedom really fictitious? Skinner answers the question with a loud and clear "yes." Let us examine his criticism in some detail.

The most popular definition of freedom is *doing what one wants to do*. The trouble with this definition, according to Skinner, is that it is based on a faulty assumption, namely, that wants are expressions of free will. A person may think that he can determine what he wants, but evidence points in the other direction: viz., a person's wants are externally determined. A person wants a drink of water because he has been deprived of it to the point of feeling thirst. He does not freely decide that he is thirsty; he is thirsty because of a certain amount of deprivation. His wanting water therefore is not an autonomous act; rather, it is determined by prior conditions. A person does not want a new car because he freely decides to want it. He wants it because of a combination of conditions: the old car is about worn out; new cars are advertised having many desirable features that his old one does not have; his wife and children pressure him to buy a new car; and so on. Conditions give rise to wants. So doing what one wants to do turns out to be determined; it is not at all the kind of freedom that one imagines.

Many processes in our culture are aimed at getting people to want certain things. For example, advertising is the art of arranging stimuli so as to predispose particular wants. Advertising is a form of classical conditioning, often called Pavlovian conditioning. It works in the following way. Any effective advertisement contains something that catches the eye, whether it is a color combination, a shape, or a novel expression. Once attention is focused on the ad, this conspicuous aspect arouses a certain feeling, such as laughter, fear, sympathy, nostalgia, sentiment, sexual attraction, or any one of the common feelings; little effort is needed to get the message. A second stimulus—namely, the product that the advertiser is trying to promote—is then associated or paired with the message. The advertisement occurs frequently because repetitions are needed to establish a reasonably strong association between the feeling and the product. Once the person is properly conditioned by the ad, his buying behavior tends to be impulsive. You can see evidence of uncritical buying in any supermarket. Many people seem to be in a kind of daze, going from one shelf to the next picking things mechanically, filling their carts without the guide of a prepared list. The cafeteria style of marketing is an ideal means for allowing conditioned wants to be satisfied.

Similarly, image makers in politics have learned that votes are gotten more effectively by conditioning feelings than by stimulating reflective thought. Political image making is not designed to arouse critical reaction; on the contrary, it is aimed at promoting uncritical acceptance of the candidate by making him *appear* ideal. Responses of people interviewed on television about their favorite political candidates suggest the effects of image making. Responses to the question of why a particular candidate is favored run pretty much as follows: "I don't know, he's just my kind of guy." "Obviously, he's better looking than the rest." "He's got that certain something." "Anyone with a smile like his is bound to be a winner." "He's the ideal American." "He seems so sincere." The interesting thing about these responses is that most people are unable to explain them. Even those reasons that the respondents think are substantial often turn out to be groundless, because they fail to differentiate between rival candidates. For example, one person may say that he likes candidate X because he promises to stop the war. But the same promise is given by other candidates. The responders usually show little evidence of having made choices by carefully looking at the evidence. Their behavior suggests, rather, that they are victims of clever conditioning or image making.

The technology of psychology contains effective ways to control what people want. Therefore, a government or powerful bloc of commercial organizations can manipulate conditions so as to get people to want certain things and not want other things. For example, preferences for music among teenagers are probably not independent of how disc jockeys and record companies behave. If the above analysis is correct, any totalitarian government should endorse the idea that freedom is doing what one wants to do, because by controlling the mass media it can pretty much determine what people want. So this popular conception of freedom does not work at all as most people assume it to work.

A second popular notion associated with freedom is: *all control of human behavior is bad.* According to Skinner, that belief conflicts with many important facts. For example, a mother restrains her young child from running into traffic. No one would judge her act as bad, yet it is clearly a form of direct control. A law makes vaccination compulsory; few people, even the champions of freedom, reject it. Compulsory education is endorsed by a large majority. It is clear that the popular adage about the evilness of all control is an exaggerated assertion.

But those who oppose Skinner insist that coercion, in general, is bad. They believe that it is particularly bad when it benefits only the controllers, and not the controlled. In short, they are against exploitation. But Skinner is also against exploitation and he is against punishment. So what is the real difference between the two positions? I think that the opponents of Skinner believe two main points: that Skinner wants to control people without their being aware of it; and that he sets himself up as the one who will decide what is good and what is bad. How does Skinner reply to that twofold claim? He says, first, that control is an integral part of life. All organisms, including man, are controlled by the environment; sometimes people are aware of being controlled and other times they are not. The environment determines behavior because it holds the key to which behavior will be rewarded and which punished. Our very lives are sustained by the environment. We do not automatically generate food within our bodies; it must be found in the environment and ingested. Some substances are nourishing and others are poisonous. We don't eat deadly mushrooms because we know their effect. Knowing a mushroom to be poisonous *determines* our leaving it uneaten. People cultivate edible plants to get needed food. The behavior required to nurture the plant is determined by the facts known about its effective husbandry. Similarly, a successful farmer cannot decide willy-nilly how to cultivate his crops. Even such a simple act as eating is determined. Food must not only be available; it must also be approached and brought to the mouth, chewed, and swallowed before its effect can be beneficial. Money is a *generalized reinforcer* (reward) because it can be used to get a variety of needed things. Wage earners must perform certain tasks before getting paid. Professional people must perform certain services before collecting fees. Control is everywhere. Sitting quietly in a room and looking around is under control because what is seen is controlled by the immediate environmental configuration. According to Skinner even an hallucination is determined by certain conditions. One cannot by an act of free will say, "Now, I am going to hallucinate and create the appearance of a black swan," and actually do what he wills. Suicide may appear to be the ultimate act of free will. But Skinner thinks otherwise. He believes that suicide is controlled by the existence of extremely aversive conditions, without which it would not occur. So any man-made design to control people does not suddenly change the world of human experience from one of freedom to one of control, because control has been there all along. Designed control is simply an effort to alter the environment so as to reduce control through chance and caprice. The control performed by physicians is not considered bad because it is used to improve and sustain health. In fact, any physician who refused to exercise his services (which are forms of control) to treat a disease would be seen as behaving in an immoral way. We pay huge sums of money to hire various expert controllers to minimize the effects of aversive conditions. We call plumbers to fix leaks and plugged drains because such conditions are aversive and they control our behavior in ways that are unpleasant. A stalled car limits or controls its owner, who hires a mechanic to control the source of trouble by eliminating it. If all controls are bad, why do we invest so much energy and resources into controlling conditions so as to yield desirable results?

The most direct kind of control is punitive. Skinner rejects such control. Instead, the most effective control is accomplished by changing something in the environment so as to produce reward after a certain kind of behavior is emitted. This is the root of behavioral engineering. Skinner simply wants to make such engineering more effective so that such miseries as pollution, the threat of nuclear war, crime, and overpopulation are minimized. Fundamentally, Skinnerian control does not emphasize direct control of people; rather it stresses a change in the control of the environment, which, in turn, will change how people behave.

Analysis along the above lines leads us to a curious and almost paradoxical observation: the champions of freedom endorse control more than they realize. Indeed, they endorse coercion by threat, whereas Skinner rejects it. For example, most anti-Skinnerians seem to endorse compulsory education, and the use of threat and punishment as means of control. Skinnerian psychology rejects such controls even in exchange for the obvious benefits that education is supposed to yield. I don't see compulsory education backed by threat in the Skinnerian system at all. Instead of aversive control, I see the conditioning of the desire to attend school by making the school environment both rewarding and useful to students. Keeping students in school by threat or punishment when school is aversive to them is quite contrary to Skinnerian principles. Students are not at fault for not liking school; it is the "fault" of the environment, which should be changed so that desirable learning is not inhibited by aversive conditions. Skinner believes in engineering a learning environment that controls the learner by reward rather than by threat, although each student might be unaware of how and why the controls work. Even permissiveness cannot obviate control.

Permissiveness as typically practiced does not work very well as a form of social engineering because it must accept whatever aversive or destructive behavior an aversive environment generates. Permissiveness per se does not change the environment to guarantee the existence of contingencies of reward on which effective learning depends. It simply changes the locus of social control from the teacher to the peer group, which may reward all sorts of unnecessary and undesirable behavior. A completely permissive environment can terrorize a timid and weak child and make a hater of him. And some of that hate may have overtones of racial prejudice, particularly if the weak child is intimidated by members of a different race.

In reply to the charge that he sets himself up as the one who is to determine what kind of behavior should or should not occur, Skinner says, in effect, that we already have enough consensus about good and bad, right and wrong, to know our objectives. Nearly all people want to reduce crime. Almost everyone is against disease. War is deemed bad along with pollution and overpopulation. We don't like poverty and the deprivations that it brings. We prefer politeness and respect to insolence and rudeness. We would rather have friends than enemies. We would like to minimize greed, cruelty, spitefulness, thoughtlessness, and the like.

The source of human misery lies in the adoption of erroneous beliefs and the use of ineffective means to implement aims. The natural environment has no investment in the welfare of the individual. It is simply there and it controls what we do. But if we study the relationships between how people act and how the environment reacts to shape behavior, we can establish effective techniques that can be used to maximize our welfare and to minimize noxious, aversive, and undesirable consequences.

To repeat, Skinner strongly rejects as false the claim that all control is bad; it cannot stand up in the face of overwhelming evidence to the contrary. And the adoption of such false notions as guides to action is bound to yield poor results. *Inefficient* use of control, on the other hand, predisposes reliance on threat and punishment, which give rise to conflict, aggression, deception, revenge, and the like.

A third popular notion is that *freedom is essentially a feeling*. Even if control prevails, it is better to feel free than not. The plausible part of the notion of freedom as feeling is that feelings are a reliable guide when applied to aversive conditions. Threat and punishment stimulate a feeling of coercion, and their absence generates a feeling of freedom.

But the weak side of the notion is that feelings are a poor indicator of freedom when reinforcers are used that have delayed aversive effects. The artful performance of a con man illustrates how feeling can mislead one into action that ends in discomfort. Unless the skill of critical evaluation is added to feeling, the person may have no defense against accepting lures that lead to delayed consequences of an unpleasant sort.

A fourth claim about freedom that Skinner rejects is that *freedom is a possession*. This claim implies that freedom is an object or thing that can be won or lost like any other piece of personal property. A person is said to lose his freedom when he comes under the control of a tyrant, and to *gain* his freedom when he frees himself of dictatorial command. Skinner says that, in fact, nothing is really gained or lost in such situations; only the environment has changed. Lack of freedom simply means that the person is under adverse constraint because of the existence of certain outer conditions. To "gain" freedom does not mean that a person acquires ownership; rather, he has simply moved from a situation of uncomfortable constraint to a new set of conditions having a relative lack of such constraint.

A CRITIQUE OF SKINNERIAN FREEDOM

I think that there are two main weaknesses in the Skinnerian argument about freedom. The first is an exaggerated dependence on the deterministic assumption. The second is the lack of importance placed on thinking. Let me examine these points in some detail.

SKINNER PLACES TOO MUCH DEPENDENCE ON DETERMINISM.

Although the deterministic assumption is reasonable, given the available facts about human behavior, it does not seem sufficient. Skinner readily admits that much operant behavior

cannot be directly connected with specific stimulus antecedents. But he contends that *changes* in a response pattern
can be demonstrated as systematically related to changes in
controlled alterations of external conditions. Indeed, he has
made many such demonstrations with rats and pigeons. It
is questionable, however, whether the great variety of human
behavior can be fully comprehended within the range of
such demonstrations.

The main crack in the tight Skinnerian system occurs
when Skinner begins to extend his principles to behavior
beyond the laboratory. He uses at least two methods to
relate his psychology to human behavior: the method of
analogy and that of extrapolation. First he sees that human
behavior is somewhat analogous to that of lower species.
The substance of the analogy seems to rest on the Darwinian
notion that animals and humans share certain common
properties with respect to body structure and functions of
vital organs. And what an animal can or cannot do rests
upon how it is put together, its body structure. So to the
extent that animals and humans share basic structures and
body functions they also share behavioral characteristics.
Skinner's line of reasoning is supported by much experimental data. The question is, just how far can the analogy
be stretched? Skinner prefers to think that it has almost unlimited bounds. But at the same time he will not be drawn
into the trap of saying that a rat is just like a human, although he has been accused of making such a claim. The
extent of comparability across species, then, remains rather
vague.

Skinner also makes many extrapolations from his laboratory data to human behavior. "Extrapolation" means to
estimate the value or significance of a variable beyond its
known range. So when Skinner extrapolates from rat-learn-
ing curves to human learning, he is assuming that the variables involved in the reinforcement event bear the same
relationships in the area of human data. Extrapolation is

similar to analogy but the two are not identical. While analogy involves the functional similarity of models (rats and humans are modeled or structured along similar lines), extrapolation is more specific and involves estimates of certain variables beyond a known range of facts. We can therefore say that Skinnerian extrapolation rests on analogy but focuses on specific factors, namely, the values in a set of variables. The weakness of operant extrapolation is that it tends to underrate the probability that the variable matrix regarding human learning is much more complex than it is on the rat level. Therefore, the complicated interaction among the human variables of learning may shift the basic relationships between reinforcement variables when contrasted with those relationships as reflected in rat data.

The fact that Skinner has not made any concerted effort to identify the variables that are peculiar to human learning, that is, beyond those found in the conditioning of rats, places his extrapolations on rather shaky grounds. His extrapolations appear sound when dealing with rather simple kinds of human learning. But when the focus is shifted to such cognitive functions as analysis, evaluation, complex judgments, synthesis of concepts, and the like, it seems well-nigh impossible to demonstrate the validity of his extrapolations. Thus, when dealing with complex actions of humans that, because of technological limitations of data gathering and lack of full knowledge of the variables involved, defy demonstrative expression, Skinner falls back on faith. His faith rests on his experience that the principles have worked in many situations before and his assumption that they should not suddenly fall apart or become useless when things become more complicated. But Skinner is probably troubled by a nagging doubt, because the substitution of faith for demonstration is not in keeping with the spirit of his system. Yet he would rather entertain doubt than adopt the categories that other psychologists use in dealing with complex behavior such as thinking, feeling, imagination, motivation, perception, and the like.

If my treatment so far is reasonably accurate, we have arrived at a legitimate point of controversy. It can be argued on good grounds that Skinner's analysis of response patterns, which extends beyond present capabilities of demonstration, can be doubted within the spirit of his psychology. We can maintain that while Skinner's logical analysis sounds plausible, it leaves the door open for entertaining other interpretations, including those based on the assumption of free choice.

Skinner may be correct. But he also may be incorrect when it comes to interpreting human behavior that falls beyond the range of experimental demonstration. Apparently, most people do not like to live with uncertainty. But it seems important to suspend judgments until we can acquire the needed information to test them properly. Certainly, Skinner is entitled to his beliefs, and to the pursuit of whatever reasonable actions he can take to further the verification of his system. It is best to look upon the struggle between Skinner and his opponents as a contest whose resolution is still in doubt, and to be willing to accept whatever compelling outcomes occur. At the moment, however, the sanest position is simply to accept the inconclusiveness of the rival arguments.

In summary, we have examined some relevant considerations which suggest that Skinner's extension of the deterministic assumption may be excessive in light of what we actually know about human behavior. Let us now turn to our second objection to the Skinnerian thesis.

SKINNER FAILS TO ACKNOWLEDGE THE FREEDOM THAT IS PRODUCED BY COGNITIVE PROCESSES.

The Skinnerian notion of freedom boils down to freedom *from* undesirable events, embracing behavior that serves to get rid of or prevent the occurrence of an aversive or unpleasant condition. It is a concept of defensive behavior that fails to cover all the useful meanings of freedom. There is another kind of behavior that is not principally defensive, but is equally convincing as a form of freedom. This behavior is largely covert; that is, it is not directly observable. It is identified as "thinking," and embraces a range of cognitive actions including analysis, evaluation, hypothesis making, and invention. Such actions manifest a kind of freedom that extends or broadens the range of possible behavior. For example, the thinking activity that resulted in unlocking atomic power opened up a vast range of applications, representing freedom *to* do things that were formerly impossible. Skinner's own psychology is another good case in point. He did not develop his psychology by simple trial-and-error-methods in the laboratory. His important decisions resulted from examining situations and data and seeing their implications and relationships. I don't see his psychology as only a set of defensive maneuvers. Yet it increases freedom to the extent that it opens up new ways of dealing with a variety of problems.

Ignorance often restricts action. Knowledge broadens the range of possible effective action. It is unlikely that the great variety of choices in modern life, produced via technology, is independent of the activity of human thought. Nor is it probable that such thought, although it has made possible a vast array of specific acts of freedom, can be reduced to defensive behavior. People are free to go from New York to London in a few hours, a freedom that did not exist until recently. The conditions that stimulated the thinking which made that freedom possible cannot simply be classed as aversive. There is a quite different stimulus to thought, namely, the awareness that the pursuit of knowledge is likely to result in positive reinforcement. Skinnerian freedom on the other hand, is cast in terms of negative reinforcement.

When a person analyzes a situation he identifies the elements that compose it. In so doing, he increases the chance of becoming aware of new patterns of the elements, new configurations that can broaden the scope of possible action. When one evaluates a proposition or process he tries to identify its positive and negative features according to some set of criteria. The evaluative process increases the possibility of creating improvements, which can also extend the range of possible action. And when a person attempts to produce hypotheses and does so successfully, he essentially produces programs of investigation that may result in the creation of a variety of new alternatives of behavior.

All constraints are not necessarily aversive. For example, the constraint imposed by gravity is not usually unpleasant, although in some situations it may be seen as aversive. But increased knowledge about gravity constituted a significant part of modern physics, which contributed to making possible the freedoms that uniquely characterize modern life.

Thought can be an instrument both of Skinner's freedoms and of the more positive freedoms mentioned above. For example, a critical analysis of a confidence game can provide the avoidance that Skinner cites. Hypothesismaking can produce effective suggestions for escaping aversive situations. But cognitive behavior can also bring into being new possibilities of behavior that extend beyond the defensive freedoms of avoidance and escape defined by Skinner. The new domains of experience so created can be seen as broadening the scope of behavior, breaking down constraints that were not formerly deemed aversive. The world of the astronaut is dramatically different from the frontiersman in early America. The difference is largely one of power, which can be seen as a medium of freedom.

CHAPTER 5

Freedom and Practice

One of the main components of the popular idea of freedom is autonomy, the notion that one is capable of generating his own goals and can carry them out despite contrary influences. This idea is pretty much the sum and substance of free will. So in this chapter the words "freedom," "autonomy," and "free will" are used interchangeably unless otherwise indicated.

The purpose of this chapter is to demonstrate the apparent need we have to cling to both freedom and determinism in the realm of practical affairs in spite of the inconsistent position that we thereby take. We live in a world in which there seems to be a continual tug of war between free will and determinism. The interaction or frequent oscillation between the need for free will and the need for determinism makes it impossible for a person to act *consistently* in terms of freedom. And, equally importantly, one cannot behave purely in accordance with determinism. Some tasks that we perform impose upon us the assumption that we must behave with a measure of autonomy, while others force us to accept that determinism is operating.

The idea that we shift frequently from a deterministic mental set to a freedom set and vice versa is fundamental to the main theme of this book, because it suggests that neither Skinner nor the most radical believers in freedom can be accepted as *generally* correct. The most defensible position is that determinism and freedom are working assumptions that we employ to fit specific experiences.

The treatment that follows about the law, morals, and religion is intended to substantiate the above claim. We shall see that any purely consistent adherence to either freedom or determinism is untenable in the practical spheres of activity.

FREEDOM AND THE LAW

Man-made laws are violable; that is, they can be disobeyed. A natural law, however, such as the law of gravity, applies to all material things; it cannot be broken. Man-made laws can be broken either through ignorance of them or by deliberate action. Thus, any violable law implies a freedom, the freedom to break it. When one breaks a civil or criminal law he is liable to punishment. The decision to punish a person for an illegal act rests on the assumption that he could have chosen to act other than he did. To execute justice, certain people are empowered to impose penalties as a means of redress, to "balance the ledger," so to speak. Legal punishment apparently is used not only to maintain some sort of balanced bookkeeping but also, apparently, to "educate" people about the desirability of law-abiding behavior. The use of punishment as a deterrent, that is, as a means of reducing the frequency of illegal acts, implies a belief that knowledge of cause-and-effect relations will have some beneficial influence on those who are tempted to break laws. This point is much debated. Evidence can be cited to support the argument that legal punishment is not an effective method of education. It is claimed that no matter how dire the threat of punishment may be, it does not prevent deliberate attempts to break the law. Also, the frequency of law-breaking has no definite correlation with the severity of threat; this can be interpreted to mean that threat does not function as a deterrent. But that interpretation is at odds with our knowledge about the behavior of avoidance. There is ample evidence to show that a perceived threat often modifies action—that one tends to avoid aversive consequences. Yet it is clear that severe threats do not always deter action. Whether or not a person deliberately decides to break a law seems to rest on what he stands to gain as against the chance of being caught and punished. If the gain is seen as very rewarding, one may try to develop a plan that minimizes the chance of getting caught while maximizing the chance of reaping the reward. Hence criminals develop professional expertise, becoming "specialists" in the art of law-breaking.

The legal concept of responsibility implies that the person is free to decide whether to break a law or not to break it. But the methods used to track down criminals operate on the assumption of determinism. A criminal's method of operation is assumed analogous to his fingerprint; it is a characteristic over which he seems to have little control. Also, when a detective attempts to match fingerprints found at the scene of a crime with known suspects, he must make the deterministic assumption. He cannot assume that a fingerprint found on a wine glass, for example, was uncaused, that it somehow got there without being touched by a human hand. The process of matching it with a suspect's prints rests on the assumption that a person's fingerprints remain constant and that when a match is discovered only one person can be responsible.

The philosophy of determinism as used in crime detection assumes that the criminal operates somewhat on the basis of compulsion, that is, he is strongly predisposed to act as he does. The background and conditions of the criminal's life impose overwhelming influences that make his behavior highly predictable. Only by making certain radical changes in the conditions under which the criminal lives can we expect much change in what he does.

The use of punishment in the law rests partly on an assumption of determinism. It would be idle to punish a person if one could not assume in doing so that somehow his behavior would be changed. But to impose punishment in the first place implies that the accused was free to act other than he did. Hence both freedom and determinism are implied in legal punishment.

One weakness in the legal concept of responsibility is revealed by psychological analysis. When the trait of responsibility is examined by some psychologists, they come up with the assertion that it amounts to nothing more than forms of behavior that accord with (implied or explicit) social expectations. For example, an employee is responsible if he does those things that are expected of him. He is irresponsible if he acts in ways contrary to expectation or to his own promises. A promise can be seen as a statement of intention to act in a certain way in the future. Essentially, it is a prediction made to one's self or to others about what line of action may be expected from the person making the promise.

When a promise is broken, one or more persons tend to suffer—those who rely upon the promise. Some broken promises, obviously, can have quite damaging consequences. But to inflict punishment on account of a broken promise does not prove the existence of freedom; it implies only that freedom is *assumed* to exist. Punishment is used to support the desire to "even the score," to deliver a punishment comparable to the hardship suffered by the victims. Yet there is no way of proving just how much freedom a person has in a choice situation, particularly *after* the act has been performed. If we believe that a person could have acted other than he did, we engage in speculation; there seems to be no way of verifying that speculation. The assumption of freedom in the law, then, cannot be validated. On the other hand, it is also impossible to prove that all behavior is determined. Hence, the paradox involved in the assumption of both freedom and determinism seems to have no unique or definite solution. It identifies a reality which somehow must be lived with.

A person who is judged insane is held not responsible under the law. But it is often difficult to determine the difference between sanity and insanity. Our methods of establishing the dividing line between sanity and insanity are very much open to question. A strong argument can be made for the assertion that a sane person's behavior is just as much determined as that of the insane. Merely to be conscious of what one is doing does not mean that he controls himself and is exempt from the influence of external conditions.

If person A attacks person B and B in turn assaults A, the law may excuse B's action as self-defense. But in another case, a person who perceives a threat that is not made overt or uttered by the aggressor may be punished for assault. Yet the causal elements are quite similar, because it can be argued that a person behaves according to the way he perceives the situation. A defendant may not be able to convince a judge or jury that he perceived a dire threat and acted accordingly. But the reality of his perception may be just as great as in the case that is clearly deemed self-defense.

In summary, it seems that judgments made in the law about freedom, responsibility, and determinism are not only inexact and therefore ridden with error but in fact rest upon assumptions which cannot be demonstrated as valid. Such areas as law, political theory, economics, anthropology, and sociology seem to operate upon certain psychological propositions accepted as axiomatic. The validity of these axioms is often questionable. Until psychology has taken the axioms as hypotheses and has demonstrated their value by convincing tests, it seems inadvisable to depend upon the social sciences to provide us with a solid foundation for deciding how society should be changed. Common sense may be as good or better than the social sciences for such decisions.

FREEDOM AND MORALS

Let us begin with some definitions, so that the use of key terms can remain clear and consistent. "Morals" will refer to standards of behavior prescribing what is right or wrong. These standards can be applied directly to samples of conduct. The extent to which actual patterns of behavior deviate from these standards is a matter of moral judgment. "Morality" stands for qualities of behavior seen as right or wrong in the abstract. For example, prevarication is a quality of verbal behavior, having relevance to a large class of assertions, that carries a negative value in many societies. Yet this judgment, which exists on an abstract level, does not always agree with morals, that is, with concrete, situation-bound standards. "It is wrong to lie to your mother" can be accepted by the same person who believes "it is right to lie to an enemy in time of war." A given moral code may be composed of many such examples that are inconsistent on the abstract level.

"Conscience" is one's own judgment of his actions and thoughts according to his moral standards. When that judgment indicates a clear difference between what one does and his morals, a feeling of stress arises that is commonly thought of as "pangs of conscience." If the person shows concern about whether or not his behavior agrees with his moral standards and if he shuns convenience in order to do what he deems right, we say that he is conscientious or that he has a strong conscience. Hence, the strength of one's conscience is inferred from one's behavior.

The above definitions are cast in the more restricted context of behavioral psychology rather than in the broader philosophical field of meaning. Their advantage lies in clarity. But the disadvantage of these relatively narrow definitions is that they tend to curtail richness of meaning. But they are sufficient for the purpose at hand, which is to point out the limitations of some popular interpretations of the relation between freedom and conscience.

One's internal or personal set of morals is not likely to agree perfectly with the prevailing or social code, which can be considered as a hypothetical average of all individual codes in a society. When the cluster of personal standards in a society converges within a narrow range, we can say that the society has a homogeneous moral system. But when the cluster is spread out, the society is morally pluralistic. As moral pluralism increases and approaches a logical extreme, it is likely that the integrity or cohesion of the society becomes threatened. Reference will be made in a later chapter to such fractionation of social values.

Does autonomy conflict with conscience, or are the two compatible? Reflection on the matter suggests that certain common notions relating to this question are superficial and misleading. If we say that conscience develops from the impact of social sanctions, as do many psychologists, we take a deterministic line of thought which suggests that "conscience" is a name given to a kind of social programming of the person for controlling his conduct. Autonomy or personal freedom appears, on the surface, to be meaningful only when one elects to flout the moral code. Only when one elects to violate a social rule does there seem to be any evidence of a behavioral sort that suggests the expression of personal freedom. Yet if one exercises such freedom, he is liable to social ostracism and to pangs of conscience that can result in a loss of freedom greater than that which is gained. This suggests that the conscience is uncompromising and that autonomy and the conscience have no way of cooperating that is constructive. Hence, autonomy seems relevant only when it is used to violate moral rules, and so long as the conscience remains in command autonomy seems to be nonfunctional. Many young people choose to act against the prevailing social code because they say that it restricts their freedom. They seem to think that they can increase their freedom only if they deviate from the common mores. So it becomes tempting to regard freedom as the opposite of conformity.

But the notion that freedom and conscience have only a negative relation in the manner described above cannot hold up in the face of some facts. For example, when it is not clear whether a given act agrees or disagrees with accepted standards, one can choose to engage in reflective analysis and estimate the likely consequences of the uncertain act. Such reflection may not only clarify what behavior is most defensible or desirable, but may also lead to some change in one's moral code. Duty cannot always be clearly determined by referring to available moral standards because the latter have a limited range.

The choice to engage in reflective thought is perhaps the most autonomous decision that one can make because it is not a matter of impulse. Nor is it something that outer conditions can compel or determine. A teacher, for example, cannot cause a student to think, although he may try to establish conditions conducive to thought. If anything that a person does is a matter of free choice, it is more probably a rational action than any other.

Simple reflexes—nonrational forms of behavior—can easily be conditioned in a deterministic way. The same is true of operant habit patterns. Feelings can also be conditioned by a systematic use of rewards and punishment. One can generate negative feelings in an acquaintance simply by treating him in a negative way. But the rational process is much harder to place under systematic control, because of the high amount of uncertainty in predicting just what chain of thought will be adopted and what conclusions will occur. Although the formulas of mathematics can be said to guide rational processes to predictable conclusions, it is questionable that much genuine thought is involved because of the rotelike pattern that is often used in following the formulas. It seems that formulas are typically used to produce answers with a minimum of reflection. Creative thinking is most likely to occur when pat formulas and prelearned channels are inadequate for reaching goals. The fact that moral formulas (codes) cannot always provide adequate guidelines for making clear-cut judgments suggests that the unavailability of a ready answer is the cue for reflective thought. It also seems probable that such thinking can produce decisions not necessarily opposed to the tenor of accepted morals. In short, it is possible that free choice can support conformity.

If reason is admitted as having a potential for constructive interaction with moral principles, the notion that conscience is only a rigid and irrational result of social sanctions cannot be fully supported. For example, one may conform to practices of sanitation because his reasoning tells him that by doing so his personal habits and his effect upon others will be more desirable than otherwise. His conformity is not a blind command of conscience. Yet his rational choice is more likely to agree with than to run counter to his conscience. Also, the deliberate decision to conform, in this case, probably strengthens his other spheres of freedom. Freedom, conformity, and rational action are not necessarily incompatible.

Social rules often contain enough latitude to accommodate a variety of individual differences. And within that zone of latitude one can exercise considerable freedom without having to reject the entire code of morals. The main inhibitor to personal freedom is not the conscience, but rather mental rigidity or lack of flexibility in modes of thinking. People of strong conscience can exhibit considerable creativity while some of weak conscience may be most rigid. Freedom is not found in blind rebellion; it is spawned by rational analysis of problems and comes to fruition in the generation of new alternatives and the testing of such alternatives.

Of course, it is possible that one's reflection can lead to the conclusion that only radical changes in one's life style can yield the kind of freedom that one deems desirable. But if one carries his thinking far enough he will be able to identify just what changes are most feasible and what plan of action is most likely to achieve those changes. This requires control over impulse and some flexibility of thought. Blind efforts to upset the status quo are likely to result in added constraints instead of increased freedom.

History suggests that people have a remarkable tolerance for aversive control. They accept all sorts of miseries with amazing passivity. Hence, the lack of critical reflection concerning the conditions of life may be a perennial phenomenon. Even under conditions of modern enlightment, with its increased tolerance of criticism and dissent, the focus is less upon rational reflection than upon party lines. Extremism tends to be associated with mental rigidity. Much of the heat and talk about freedom may have little relationship with cognitive independence on an individual level. So the most noisy crusaders for freedom are likely to be among the easiest victims of a totalitarian innovation.

The upshot of these considerations is that autonomy may have a much weaker appeal for most people than is implied by the lip service given to it. The acceptance of autonomy is not likely to be a wholehearted one because of stubborn facts that accord with determinism and because of conflict of motives. It seems self-evident that social pressures have a causal relation with many patterns of behavior. And the apparent need for security, environmental stability, and some measure of routine action may not accord with the desire for maximum independence. Therefore, the basic problem is how to create the kind of freedom that does not result in excessive sacrifice of those useful practices that accord with determinism. Again, the most compelling conclusion is that even in the moral realm neither complete determinism nor complete freedom promises the best results. Some combination of the two, some concept that denotes interaction between independence and conformity, is probably needed. No practical and viable solution seems possible by adopting either extreme.

FREEDOM AND RELIGION

The issue regarding human freedom from the religious standpoint boils down to arguments about the nature of both God and man. If man has freedom, God is limited in knowledge; that is, He cannot know in advance just what decisions a person will make. This means that God is not omniscient (all-knowing). On the other hand, if God is all-knowing, that is, if he knows all events from the beginning of time to infinity, He must know just what each person will do, including all decisions he will make. In that case, man is not free, since he must act in accordance with God's perfect knowledge. And if God has perfect knowledge, thus making man's life predestined, the basic relationship between God and man becomes questionable. The Judeo-Christian doctrine seems to say that man's relationship with God is one of worship, adoration, awe, respect, and willing obedience. But if man is predestined in all that he does, he is programmed also in his relation toward God. So if he worships God, he does so because he cannot do otherwise; his behavior is predetermined. Hence the worship of God is robbed of its significance and merit.

If God is incapable of sin, He lacks the freedom to choose evil. But then a supposedly perfect being is limited and in one respect is inferior to free men, who can exercise choice as between good and evil. But to regard man as superior to God even in respect of the dubious honor of having the ability to choose evil over good is to invert the God-man relationship. Religious tradition seems to demand that God must be superior to man in every respect.

The original sin of man, according to the Judeo-Christian belief, was an affront to God because man chose to exercise freedom of choice rather than to remain strictly obedient. And freedom of choice must include the possibility of choosing evil over good. If man had not sinned he would have remained obedient to God, but in doing so he would have sacrificed freedom. Because man is a creature inferior to God, his judgment was prone to error. Original sin was the decision to exercise freedom of judgment, which is fraught with error when practiced by creatures of less than perfect wisdom. If man had remained strictly obedient to God, man would have been unfree. While the decision to become free meant that man would sin because of his imperfect wisdom, it also suggested that he would experience learning by reaping knowledge produced by the consequences of his choices. Sin, knowledge, and freedom are all wrapped in the same package.

Perhaps the most serious crime that man committed when he chose to be free was the implied desire to become like

God, to become God's equal instead of His servant. The central theme of original sin is played over and over in the history of the family. When the child reaches adolescence, he tends to challenge the authority of his parents; he wants to make his own decisions. He feels that his own judgment is as good as and often superior to that of his parents, who, he believes, are particularly ignorant about the psychology of the new generation. The adolescent becomes wedded to freedom when he entertains doubts about parental authority and seeks to explore, choose, and learn by exercising his own judgment. He makes many mistakes, but he also has a good chance of equaling or surpassing the wisdom of his parents. The assertion of independence of the adolescent is perhaps the foundation of social change.

If original sin meant the choice of freedom to learn by man's own experience over blind obedience to God, it must be seen as producing the kind of challenge to God that was blasphemous. The decision to be free meant that man decided to strike out on his own, pretty much like the adolescent. In choosing freedom over obedience, man challenged God's authority and sought to create and harness power on his own. He has come a long way, judging from the results of science and technology. But Western religions suggest that man's decision to make it on his own will end in a gigantic failure and that he must return to God if he is to save himself. In returning to God, however, man must again make himself subservient, and he must sacrifice his freedom before he can reap the benefits of God's wisdom. Man's experiment with freedom has been a noble but tragic odyssey, particularly in the application of science. Scientific knowledge, having been translated into power through technology, now threatens to exterminate man, thus justifying God's wisdom expressed before the fall. The humanists, who are now so militant against science, cannot resolve the problem because their doctrine is too man-centered; it still supports original sin by using freedom as a basic value.

There is now a serious reconsideration of the notion that man cannot survive without having a proper relationship with God. But much of organized religion, particularly those churches that follow intellectual theology, seems to substitute humanism for religion. Modern theology has definitely turned against predestination and has taken the side of freedom, which implies a limitation of God's knowledge. It has become humanistic, and in doing so it has supported a man-centered set of values that tends to diminish the role of God. The humanistic solution to the problems of modern society appears no better than scientific ones; indeed, it appears even less plausible because it tends to involve suppression of the growth of scientific knowledge. The ignorance among humanists about science is often far greater than the ignorance of humanism among scientists. It is impossible to achieve even an adequate understanding of the problems of the modern world without scientific knowledge. This does not mean that man has changed his nature nor that a study of the classics is irrelevant to modern social relationships. But it does mean that such problems as pollution, overpopulation, and nuclear war cannot be grasped very well by one ignorant of science.

A state of absolute obedience to God's laws would mean that man's freedom *to* err would be eliminated while his freedom *from* error would be increased. Obedience to God, therefore, does not mean that all freedom is denied man, although a common interpretation of the problem holds that freedom to err is the only freedom. But if man is born in sin, he automatically has the freedom to err, thus making strict obedience to God virtually impossible. If man is born in sin and cannot resist it, man's justification in God's mind must occur without imposition of the impossible demand for strict obedience. Therefore, man's justification before God must occur by divine grace rather than by any special merit earned by the person. If that is true, predestination again assumes central importance.

The upshot of the argument on freedom and religion is to leave it in a state of paradox. Acceptance of man's freedom imposes limitations on God's knowledge, which is incompatible with a perfect being. Acceptance of predestination, however, undercuts the meaning of worship because there seems to be no value in worship as performed by an automaton. Determinism is needed to uphold the notion that God is the author of all power, that all events are under His control. Determinism is also necessary to support the concept of God as omniscient, knowing in advance what is going to happen down to the minutest detail. If such is the case, predestination must be accepted. On the other hand, freedom to err must be accepted in order to make any sense of worshipping God. But if man is born with the freedom to err, it seems impossible for him to obey God's laws, because sin is a part of his heritage, a genetic aspect of his being. If that is true, however, it would be idle to judge him as deficient in the eyes of God, who is supposed to be the author of justice.

The gist of the religious paradox is that both freedom and determinism are needed to support the traditional Judeo-Christian doctrine. Religion assumes that man needs a relationship with a superior power, that he cannot make it on his own. The problems that religion embraces involve the knotty decisions of how to define the superior power and man's proper relation to that power. The Judeo-Christian tradition apparently has not been successful in resolving these issues in a way that is compatible with the modern temper.

CONCLUSION

The thesis of this chapter is that practical systems, including the law, morals, and religion, require a belief in both freedom and determinism. This position implies that such a belief is crucial to psychological health. Self-autonomy or free will is needed as a working assumption to protect one from complete passivity, a dysfunctional state that accompanies such mental diseases as catatonia. Belief in a measure of autonomy seems necessary to the coping process. If a person were absolutely convinced that he really had no options, that whatever he might decide to do must end in naught, that all his effort to translate desire into concrete action must inevitably fail, he would probably have scant motivation or drive. He would have no hope and would probably capitulate to the point that his existence would be cut short. So it seems that psychological health pretty much requires a belief in and the exercise of some measure of autonomy.

On the other hand, psychological health also requires awareness of conditions beyond one's personal control. One must regard himself as dependent upon certain conditions that operate independently of his whims, desires, and power. The spinning of the earth on its axis, the movement of the earth around the sun, the dynamics of weather, the basic life processes—all these plus countless other phenomena occur regardless of one's feelings, opinions, and personal desires. If one loses awareness of such things and comes to think that the universe is under his power, the delusion will be correlated with loss of effectiveness in the social community. His sanity will be questioned.

So it seems that normal development of the human being requires acceptance of two logically incompatible beliefs: self-autonomy and environmental determinism. Neither one can be accepted while excluding the other completely without crippling consequences. Even in science it is not desirable to operate solely on a deterministic basis. Some events in life yield the best returns when we behave as if we were autonomous. Other experiences are more usefully associated with environmental determinism. Personal welfare requires frequent shifts between the two assumptions according to the nature and purpose of the situations and tasks we face.

If survival requires a pragmatic compromise between the two concepts, and if Skinner holds survival as the ultimate value, it would seem that this system would become more serviceable if it reflected that practical compromise. My opinion is that Skinner's own behavior implies the exercise of autonomy, a personal belief by him that his decisions are not purely the result of external forces. His behavior seems to me to reflect strong hope, a desire to use his influence to spread acceptance of his techniques and principles. If he had been perfectly passive, the result of the logical extreme of the belief in environmental determinism, few if any of us would ever have heard of operant psychology. Indeed, it is hard to imagine that any of his contributions would have occurred. I think that Skinner senses the usefulness and necessity of autonomy—although it may be impossible to explain —because his notions of self-control and operant behavior do not rule out free will completely. Despite the fact that he rejects free will as inoperative in a scientific system, the loopholes in his notions of self-control and operant behavior allow for a sub rosa acceptance of autonomy. I strongly suspect that self-autonomy is a necessary assumption for applying the principles of operant psychology and for applying any other set of scientific principles.

Skinner seems to say that self-autonomy is a fiction that has no functional importance in the science of human behavior. I think that there is a contradiction in that position. Even if we admit that self-autonomy may be an illusion or fiction, we can hardly deny that the fiction has practical importance. Let us agree that belief in autonomy is simply the result of a particular history of reinforcement and that it becomes a strong belief after it has been intermittently reinforced. It therefore becomes a part of a pattern of behavior that is probably diffused across a broad repertoire of action. Autonomy is expressed within awareness as a belief that one's initiative is real and yields useful returns. It is correlated with the fact that parts of the environment can be controlled by the person and that the results of that control are often useful. Therefore, the *belief* in autonomy is an integral part of the behavior that has been conditioned in a certain way. And it is improbable that the belief in autonomy could be extinguished without also extinguishing the associated parts of the pattern, that is, those parts that involve initiative and that yield important outcomes. In other words, if a person's belief in autonomy could be extinguished, it is likely that he would become so passive that he would exhibit symptoms of psychosis. And so if belief in self-autonomy is an integral part of the kind of behavior that operant psychology attempts to strengthen, namely, contingency patterns initiated by operant action, it seems essential to accept the fiction of autonomy as a necessary aspect of healthy behavior. Consequently, it appears that Skinner's desire to extinguish belief in autonomy may be self-defeating.

The upshot of all these considerations is that there is no psychological incompatibility between environmental determinism and autonomy, although the two concepts are logically divergent.

part Three

PSYCHOLOGICAL FREEDOMS AND EDUCATION

CHAPTER 6

Three Psychological Freedoms

The purpose of this chapter is to elaborate upon the meaning of cognitive freedom and to show that it lies outside the concept of freedom used by Skinner. The intent is to point out that the cognitive type of freedom is a legitimate form and that it yields a special kind of utility that cannot be found in the Skinnerian account. As indicated below, the idea is cast in a psychological frame of reference along with two other freedoms that are related to the cognitive notion in that all three can be expressed as basic needs which must be satisfied in the process of normal human development.

Perhaps most data that psychologists study refer to three classes of human activity: feeling, knowing, and acting. That is an oversimplification of the facts, but it is sufficiently correct for the purpose at hand. I want to identify some psychological freedoms and to examine them from the standpoint of human growth and development.

The term "feeling" is a common word that will be used to identify the domain of affect, roughly the emotional side of human nature. "Knowing" will stand for all cognitive activities, including thinking, problem solving, and other rational processes. "Acting" refers to physical behavior and particularly to all response classes comprising operant behavior.

In order to generate the concepts of the psychological freedoms, let us assume that freedom is the absence of anything that obstructs, blocks, or impedes a preferred or natural course of action. By using this notion of freedom and by connecting it with the psychological areas of feeling, knowing, and acting, we can develop three psychological freedoms that may cover most of human activity. With these thoughts in mind, let us move directly to the three freedoms.

PHYSICAL FREEDOM— FREEDOM OF MOVEMENT

Jails, mental hospitals, concentration camps, and the like are designed to limit freedom of physical movement. Walls, fences, "No Trespassing" signs, hedges, door locks, and other devices are also used to restrict movement. Roads, sidewalks, and learned patterns of action serve to regulate movement within certain limits. Restrictions on movement are imposed to provide a workable distribution of physical freedom. Traffic signals, caution lights, and speed-limit signs regulate the tempo of traffic flow so that the channels of movement remain functional.

The existence of a need for freedom of movement can be inferred from the high activity rate of young children and the negative reaction they show when movement is constricted. Children who have been imprisoned in attics, closets, sheds, and cellars typically show severe retardation in development. The need for a certain amount of stimulation has been well documented. Physical movement not only produces internal stimulation for response chaining in the learning of motor skills but also introduces the person to a wide variety of external stimuli, necessary for increasing the range of experience. While physical movement represents a basic need, its regulation is also necessary when available space is limited, as in ghettos and busy commercial areas.

As population density increases, the problem of how to regulate physical movement becomes increasingly difficult. The choice is not between imposing or not imposing limitations on movement, because increased population density itself creates restrictions. It is probable that no combination of rules governing physical movement can be satisfactory when population density reaches a certain level. The psychological need for unencumbered space seems particularly important to the American life style because so much time is spent in traveling during the work day and during free time. The amount of real space required to meet the psychological needs of a given society depends somewhat on established traditions and on how the society manages its technological systems; in general, the level of affluence found in a society is probably a rough index to determine the threshold of overcrowding. The optimal number of people per square mile cannot be known until many other facts are taken into consideration. A society that depends upon hunting animals for food probably needs several square miles per person to sustain life. Another society that depends mainly upon agriculture, however, needs space according to the fertility of land. But where farming is mechanized and there is plenty of rich land, it is possible to support more people in metropolitan areas than is psychologically healthy. Our knowledge about psychological space, scant though it is, remains unused, and we continue to glut cities without regard to the life style we wish to maintain and without recognition of the mental and emotional stresses that ensue.

Frustration of movement imposed by man-made barriers, including increased population, is rising and forces changes in common response patterns. Whether or not the pressure generated will exceed the capacity of people to make adequate adjustment may be hard to determine. But there seems little doubt that the trend of increased crowding will multiply our psychological problems.

Perhaps the most popular notion of freedom is doing what one pleases so long as no one is injured or harmed. This idea is usually coupled with the belief that the human being has an inherent right to such freedom. And it implies that physical movement is a valuable part of human freedom. The notion also suggests that the person has a right to free choice of a vocation and lifestyle, free selection of a mate, and production of a family without imposed restrictions. But as these freedoms are exercised, it becomes increasingly difficult to determine just which acts satisfy the criterion of freedom of not harming anyone. For example, exercising the freedom to determine one's family size could eventually produce a population density that would impose severe limitations on individual freedom. The critical assumption behind this definition of freedom that makes it questionable is that the person can determine, at the time of choosing among alternatives, all the important consequences that will flow from his action. Such an assumption is particularly weak in a society that fails to emphasize a habit of thoughtful analysis prior to making choices. No society has yet stimulated the development of sufficient skills to cope with the pragmatic criterion adequately, that is, to discern the important consequences of actions in advance and to make decisions accordingly.

A person who decides to use drugs and later becomes an

addict may sincerely believe that no harm is imposed on others because of his decision. But despite his sincerity, there is a good probability that he will be wrong. Unfortunately, most persons lack the knowledge and wisdom to judge in advance all the important consequences that a decision may have. The accumulation of errors resulting from faulty choices may serve to restrict severely the freedom of persons in future generations.

EMOTIONAL FREEDOM

Anxiety, guilt, fear, dread, and despair are some of the common undesirable emotional states. According to many psychologists, they arise from stresses and inhibitions which tend to block or restrict the expression of natural instincts. Young children, neurotics, and psychotics are probably unaware of the actual causes of their aversive feelings. The events that precipitate anxiety, for example, are not always clearly discerned, because expereiences that have been forgotten can have delayed effects. A person may feel anxious when faced with a decision because of a traumatic incident in his past. Memory of the episode may be repressed but its negative consequences arise when the person faces a decision that is unconsciously associated with the traumatic event. Inhibitions that arise from acceptance of a severe moral code may likewise have delayed consequences that produce emotional conflicts. In general, stress and frustration suggest a lack of emotional freedom.

Many psychologists think that a certain amount of emotional freedom is necessary for normal development. Such freedom is taken as the absence of excessive inhibition to the expression of feelings. The child who is spontaneous readily shows his feelings, but the child under severe stress may assume a variety of defenses to camouflage his fears.

The psychological importance of spontaneity may be connected with the utility of candidness. The candid person usually behaves so that his intent is quite clear. Other people can usually adjust to him without undue complications. But the devious person who carefully camouflages his intent tends to generate misunderstanding and uneasiness in others. As a parent, this person is likely to influence his children to become devious, oblique, and deceptive, thus multiplying the psychological problems in his social environment.

Emotional freedom is not an autonomous product of one's own free will. The child, for example, is not in a position to decide freely whether or not he is going to be spontaneous. His emotional pattern is pretty much a result of how older people, particularly his parents, treat him. Emotional freedom is influenced by the wisdom, decisions, and actions of older people during childhood. They must protect the child from unnecessary stress, act as desirable models, and adopt rather stable and predictable ways of behaving.

Psychonanalysis is a method for trying to identify the causes of excessive anxiety and bringing those causes to the awareness of the patient. When the patient is made properly aware of the cause, it is assumed that he will be able to complete the therapy by making a realistic adjustment, which apparently cannot be made so long as the cause is unknown. Successful therapy increases emotional freedom by reducing the anxiety caused by excessive inhibition imposed on certain instincts. Such emotional freedom is considered necessary for a healthy ego and for good adjustment to reality.

Efforts to protect emotional freedom find their most practical expression in the movement called mental hygiene, which is concerned with locating and controlling conditions that produce excessive stress. One effect of stress is apparently a blockage of normal emotional expression. Frustration that is not balanced by an adequate outlet of energy creates internal pressures that produce lesions through which energy seeps. But the balance so achieved is unsatisfactory and the person remains in an abnormal state of tension. Emotional freedom is partially under the control of the person but, according to Freud, is mostly the result of determinants beyond conscious control. So the best means of realizing adequate emotional freedom is through proper nurture, which maintains a margin of stress that acts to produce change, development, and maturation but that does not become excessive. Spontaneity, openness, warmth, and empathy are some of the traits which indicate that emotional freedom is adequate.

Emotional freedom does not depend upon a negation of determinism. There are determinants of emotional freedom just as there are causes of its absence.

COGNITIVE FREEDOM

The solution of many problems depends upon possession of adequate information. A person ignorant about medicine cannot treat diseases as effectively as a physician. One who has no knowledge of mathematics has no freedom to handle problems requiring such knowledge. An illiterate person has no freedom to read and to manipulate printed or written symbols; his cognitive freedom in everyday matters is severely restricted. Cognitive freedom is also limited by such conditions as restricted access to information and distribution of misleading or false information as in propaganda, many public relations practices, and much advertising..

Cognitive freedom is increased by effective learning or education. The student who acquires a grasp of some body of knowledge gains the necessary information for dealing with a variety of problems. His ability to apply his knowledge, however, may be quite limited because skill in application is not guaranteed simply by success in acquiring knowledge. It follows that education ought to promote both acquisition of information and skill in its application in order to broaden the range of effective action open to a person.

The game of chess, for example, requires knowledge about the rules of the game plus skill in inductive reasoning, which, of course, must be applied within the rules. Chess is a game of competition in which each player tries to limit the freedom of movement of the other with the object of bringing checkmate to the opponent; checkmate means total loss of freedom for the loser. The two players begin with virtually the same amount of freedom. As the game progresses the number of options become astronomical. Probably no player is capable of identifying all possible combinations. A player's freedom to select strong moves is limited by his ability to analyze the consequences of the options that he can discern on any given play. Ability to look ahead with accuracy is the basis of exercising cognitive freedom in the game. Each player tries to increase the number of desirable options open to him while limiting the alternatives available to his opponent. Success depends almost entirely on a certain kind of cognitive skill; chance plays a minor role. The game, however, is not only a battle of inductive reasoning but also a kind of psychological warfare largely amounting to ways and means of disconcerting one's opponent within the limits of the rules. In championship contests this sort of gamesmanship seems to be a significant factor. But no player can advance to the ranks of top competition without great cognitive skill.

Chess offers a particularly good context for speaking about cognitive freedom because it is not complicated by conditions that camouflage or override the importance of cognitive skill. In everday life the importance of cognitive freedom can be easily de-emphasized and underrated. Chance or luck often seems to have a significant bearing on one's success.

One's unconscious motives, attitudes, feelings, somewhat accidental occurrences in the social environment, and a variety of other unpredictable events can be associated with outcomes. These noncognitive elements often attract more attention than they may merit. In chess those factors are minimized and the person is faced with the problem of how to protect the freedom of movement of his own pieces while limiting that of the opposing pieces. He can depend little upon luck. There is no throwing of dice, no drawing of cards, no fortuitous events that can serve as a basis for hope.

The kind of freedom found in chess bears a slight similarity to the existential notion of freedom. Within both models, one is on his own. He must make decisions and accept the responsibility for the consequences. Whatever excuses he may make can give him little comfort, because he alone decides what to do. There are no complicating circumstances that compel one to act other than he chooses within the rules of the game. His only resources are his own initiative and skill; he may be outclassed by his opponent. He has to live with the fact of defeat when that occurs; he has no teammates to blame.

One main difference between the chess model of freedom and the existentialist model is that the latter places little value on rational reflection as a means of dealing with problems. Freedom in chess is accumulated as a result of increasing skill in inductive thinking. Existential freedom, however, seems to be a condition in which the person finds himself and if he is sensitive to the nature of his existence he has a compelling awareness of his freedom. His problem is what to do with the freedom he has. In chess freedom is given in a certain amount at the start of the game. Its gain or loss directly results from the decisions one makes and how they compare with the decisions of his opponent.

When cognitive freedom is contrasted with freedom of movement and emotional freedom, some interesting differences emerge. The barriers to movement are physical in nature and tend to condition movement into channels that are relatively clear of obstruction. In cities, especially, the movement of people is similar to that of rats in mazes. A view of a city from a helicopter shows the maze pattern quite clearly. Automobiles and pedestrians move in lanes that intersect, and some lanes terminate in dead ends. Hallways and other open spaces in buildings are channels in which narrow lanes of opposing traffic follow "grooves" so as to allow maximum freedom. While it is probable that people also *think* in channels carved by habit, cognitive freedom has the advantage over freedom of movement in that the activities of thinking, daydreaming, and imagining contain no physical barriers. One can imagine something that does not exist. Yet one may also translate the imagined object into reality by bringing together those real elements that correspond to the symbolic components of his thought. The development and use of concepts can often provide the springboard for overcoming physical restrictions. Thus, the latitude found in thought is often a necessary prelude to the alteration of conditions so as to realize increased freedom of movement. The technology which has produced new modes of transportation (trains, automobiles, airplanes, steamships, balloons, submarines, rockets) that give increased freedom of movement on land, in water and air, and through outer space depends basically upon cognitive activity. Without some workable *concept* of an airplane, it seems impossible to account for its development as a physical reality. Thus, cognitive creations have real consequences for freedom of movement.

Obviously, technology has also served to limit freedom of movement by supplying an overabundance of devices which encumber space, particularly in urban areas. Also, technology has produced conditions for rapid growth of population by diminishing infant mortality, prolonging the average life span, and making food plentiful. At this point, the negative effects of technology are apparently outweighing the positive. Yet the problems so created may require even more imaginative technologies rather than curtailment of technology in general.

The psychological freedoms of movement, emotion, and cognition are probably interdependent. Unless the need for unconstricted movement is met the child's growth may be stunted and he may fail to develop normal emotions and good ability to learn and think. If too much stress limits his emotional freedom, his range of movement and thought will probably be restricted. And if the constraints to cognitive freedom are excessive he will probably fail to mature emotionally and exercise freedom of movement in normal ways.

Physical movement is limited by the conditions that surround the child. And he does not say to himself that he ought to express emotional freedom for the good of his mental health. Conscious choice seems to play a scant role in the growth of both of these freedoms, particularly in the life of the child. But cognitive freedom is a different matter. Becoming aware of alternatives, the person anticipates the consequences of different choices. As the child grows in ability to think about the merits and probable consequences of different options, he tends to delay impulsive action by interposing cognitive deliberation. He *thinks* about the choices open to him. And his thought can often change the course of action. The thinking person goes out of his way to collect information that is not immediately available. He uses the information to construct different options. And he makes a choice that is probably quite different from that which he would have made if he had not stoped to deliberate. It is not so much the act of choice per se that is most characteristic of cognitive freedom, but rather the collection and manipulation of information to build options. The choice itself may be influenced by how one feels or by some other nonrational force. But without the intervention of thought, the scope of available alternatives from which to choose may be very restricted.

Deliberation broadens the latitude of action. And that is the essence of freedom. It is difficult if not impossible to prove that choice itself is undetermined. And under some conditions it is impossible to prove that choice is determined, because no clear-cut determinants can be identified. The issue about just how free the act of choosing is may permanently resist any general and absolute answer. But unless the person is aware of alternatives it is meaningless to speak of free choice. The building of options through deliberation creates the possibility of free choice, and allows one to feel that one is not constrained solely by what is immediately given.

Awareness of a constraint serves to stimulate thought, which, as we have seen, often results in increasing the number of alternatives. Thus, the creation of alternatives depends on awareness of constraint. Thought, stimulated by constraint, can devise ways of overcoming the barrier and hence can increase freedom. This line of reasoning suggests that freedom and constraint are not independent of one another. Problem solving requires the awareness of some barrier that restricts action. Being conscious of a barrier, one is stimulated to surmount or work around it. Thinking, planning, and deliberation are simply names for the process of building possible ways of overcoming barriers.

It is not the *use* of freedom itself that is most satisfying. Many freedoms are taken for granted. The freedom to select food in a cafeteria, the freedom to watch events at a distance via TV, the freedom to travel hundreds of miles in a few hours, etc., are commonplace. As these freedoms are taken for granted, they lose the freshness and intensity with which they were first experienced; we become satiated. The most rewarding aspect of freedom lies in the overcoming of constraints and barriers that makes the exercise of freedom possible by widening the range of possible action, and this is an activity that requires the use of cognitive skills. Development of such skills, then, is necessary in order to enjoy this most valuable aspect of freedom.

Although Skinnerian freedom is an important part of the larger concept, without cognitive freedom the former would amount to no more than primitive patterns of avoidance and escape. It does not seem possible to describe cognitive freedom in purely deterministic terms.

CHAPTER 7

Cognitive Freedom
and Education

FURTHER ASPECTS OF FREEDOM

Freedom is a variable. The amount of freedom that a person has at a given time depends upon two conditions: the pressure imposed by the situation and his skill in devising alternatives for action. If one is awakened in his home after it is half-consumed by fire, his choices are quite restricted. If a person is threatened by a blackmailer, his range of alternatives may be narrow, although greater than in the previous example. When one is shopping for a new home, the number of decisions is usually considerable. While the environment initially limits the scope of useful alternatives, the only working choices are those within the awareness of the person. One has the potential to develop much skill in becoming aware of choices. One's range of freedom depends upon how well one develops that potential. So the freedom that two people enjoy in identical situations may be quite different. One's functional freedom is a matter of how one puts his abilities to work in formulating possibilities and selecting a plan of action. Yet situations obviously differ in the number and kinds of constraints imposed on the person. Cognitive freedom is most dramatically expressed when constraints seem overwhelming and yet effective means of coping with them are invented and used. We are not particularly concerned here with such dramatic instances; rather, our focus will be on the features and uses of cognitive freedom and how they relate to education.

Skinner is correct in claiming that what a person does is influenced by the situation. But he does not emphasize sufficiently the individual differences in skill and ingenuity among people. He believes that if we want young people to become inventive and flexible, we can achieve this by setting goals and by managing reinforcement so as to shape these skills. But it is not clear in his prescription just how reflective thought or other cognitive skills are established. His prescription for changing covert behavior is to follow the same formula as is used for shaping overt behavior. But in fact shaping in his system is limited to overt acts, and the effect on covert behavior such as thinking is assumed to occur as a correlate of observable performance.

The most significant behavior, according to Skinner, is observable and has some direct effect on the environment; in other words, it is operant behavior. He seems to place little importance on thinking as a prelude to action. He advocates the shaping of verbal behavior via reinforcement, hence implying that logical analysis can be so shaped when reasoning is expressed by verbal statements; that is, logical thinking patterns can be shaped by skillful management of cueing and feedback. In general, any abstract relationship can be taught if it can be presented in physical terms and if the proper reinforcement is used. It is doubtful, however, that those conditions are always necessary for effective learn-ing of relationships. For example, some higher-order mathe-matical relationships seem to defy representation in physical terms, and yet they are learned by many people.

Freedom is fluid because it changes continually as the person moves from one situation to another. The population of alternatives is fixed by the environment in a given situa-tion and a new population emerges when conditions change. Also, the adequacy of one's analysis changes across condi-tions. For example, a skilled politician may compete well in discussions concerning political issues. But when dealing with technical computer problems his flexibility may drop to zero.

PASSIVE FREEDOM

Passive freedom is the kind associated with habit, which has been discussed before. The freedom involved in habit occurs when no barriers block the free flow of routine action. When one is crippled by a muscle spasm or partial paralysis he vividly appreciates the many acts that he ordinarily does with the ease of habit. The freedom produced by habit is passive because it requires little or no initiative to set it in motion. But habit is also confining, in the sense that it is rigid and directs behavior within narrow channels. When habit dominates nearly all of one's actions one is likely to be dubbed as "set in his ways," and is likely to exhibit little ingenuity or creative behavior. If the environment is quite stable and habit is sufficient to sustain a tolerable existence, the person is likely to enjoy only passive or routine freedom.

ACTIVE FREEDOM

Active freedom occurs within the Skinnerian perspective, that is, when the person does something to avoid or escape an aversive situation. While some avoidance and escape behavior, such as sneezing, may be a matter of reflex action or automatic response, much freedom requires reflective thought. Getting rid of an undesirable political leader through the democratic process is a manifestation of active freedom that requires more than automatic reflexes. Active freedom in the Skinnerian sense is defensive and depends upon awareness of some threat or undesirable condition. Freedom is produced by any action that is instrumental in getting rid of the aversive condition.

CREATIVE FREEDOM

Creative freedom is more than defensive action. It is the process of deliberate search for new alternatives and may have little to do with avoidance or escape. It is perhaps best regarded as invention. The invention of the airplane, for example, can hardly be confined within the limits of defensive behavior. In fact, the development of the airplane was a deliberate confrontation with risks and dangers that could have been easily avoided simply by ignoring the sweat and trouble in trying to conquer the air. Space travel required many inventions before astronauts could risk their lives to explore other planets. There was no pressing need to devise successful space ships merely to escape some threat or punishment. The problems and dangers opened up by space travel suggest that some people seek freedom to explore even when the new territory may be fraught with hidden dangers and perhaps inevitable disasters. There is no doubt that the inventions necessary to provide space travel produced a kind of freedom, but something quite different from the defensive freedom defined by Skinner.

Successful invention usually expands freedom of action or range of influence and it is pursued even when it is not clear just what advantages will ensue. Invention often leads to new problems, some of which can be clearly predicted during the inventive process. But it is often rewarding even though it may create more problems and aversive conditions than it solves or alleviates.

Invention is an aspect of creativity that cuts across all fields of activity. The novelist invents or creates some unique pattern of characters, situations, and action. Painters, poets, and gadget makers are inventors. The researcher invents when he develops a problem, and crystallizes it into some hypothesis or question, and decides how to pursue its exploration. In doing so, he may discover new problems and abandon his initial one. His inventions may come to naught, but he is likely to persist in his efforts, partly because invention tends to be rewarding.

The expression of creative freedom not only involves invention but frequently depends also upon the ability to analyze and criticize the status quo, to reject or ignore the press of popular opinion, and to formulate problems and questions that may be alien to existing custom. The inventor is often a good critic of the status quo, but he does not become fixated in the habit of carping. He takes the next step of using his abilities to create promising alternatives that are often beyond the awareness of the masses. His creations may be quickly adopted, or they may arouse active rejection and be only slowly accepted.

The creative person usually has a quite different style of life from that of the ordinary person. Somehow he is relatively independent of the rewards that seem to influence most people. It is hard to fit him into the Skinnerian perspective without using questionable or untestable interpretations of his action. Skinner, himself, has pursued the inventive life, and his behavoir does not seem to fit neatly into the psychological scheme that he has proposed.

It may be too much to expect that education can shape creativity. But it is not excessive to expect that some of its characteristics can be promoted, particularly resistance to pressures that inhibit independent thinking. The sheeplike behavior of the masses has both advantages and disadvantages. Its advantages lie in the production of unity that makes for a tolerable routine life. But its main disadvantage is its tendency to render the individual rather helpless in becoming aware of and resisting popular pressures when those pressures invite bad consequences. The almost total lack of ability on the part of teenagers to resist peer-group influences is a good example of how uncritical followership inhibits the expression of independence.

Before I attempt to suggest how education may help students to acquire a healthy balance of independence and cooperativeness, let us look at some of the characteristics of education in the American public schools.

EDUCATION

The American school contains facilities to help students learn information and certain skills. It is reasonably effective in promoting its aims, provided the student has the proper motivation, attitudes, and potential. But if these are incompatible with the aims and processes of instruction, the school is not likely to succeed in terms of its own philosophy and purposes.

Much attention and effort have been given to the education of the whole child. But the task usually fails if the child's background is not in harmony with the direction in

which the school is prepared to move him. Entire personalities cannot be effectively reshaped on any planned basis
in our public schools because the kinds of influences needed
to do it are simply not found there. The school cannot compete with forces in the community and in peer groups when
those forces are incompatible with educational efforts.

In earlier times the school was a major source of information. But with the growth of the mass media, the school no
longer functions as such. Its main service is to help students
process and use the growing amount of data that is readily
available from other sources. The availability of information
per se, does not guarantee its effective use. The student
needs to learn how to select information, how to analyze it,
how to identify its valuable implications, and how to use it
effectively in making decisions. The mass media are not
managed so as to promote these aims because they are usually controlled by people motivated by profit. The profit
motive is not always compatible with promoting the cognitive freedom of consumers.

Some critics of education have correctly noted that the
learning of information is no longer the vital function of the
school. But many of these critics have incorrectly assumed
that the whole area of cognitive development can be safely
ignored in favor of the areas of attitudes, feelings, emotions,
social sensitivities, improvement of the self-concept, and
other somewhat noncognitive aspects of human development. But when education is devoted mainly to the improvement of the noncognitive parts of the personality it runs into
insurmountable problems, because the human personality is
still a dark continent in the world of knowledge. Theories of
personality are multiple and conflicting. They are marked by
ambiguities and mushy notions which can account for almost
anything, and hence for hardly anything with any assurance.
The reliable substance that useful theories need for practical
application has not yet been developed in the study of the

human personality. The various theories are quite stimulating and they provide many interesting notions and suggestions, but they do not have the validity necessary for direct applicability to education.

The most damaging influence of personality theories is likely to occur when teachers assume the truth of one and reject the others, when they doggedly use a pet theory without examining it critically. The unfortunate results of some sensitivity training, for example, demonstrate how discipleship in this area can be dysfunctional.

One good use of theories of personality is to help teachers acquire flexibility in observing and interpreting personality phenomena. And perhaps the most valuable use they provide is as sets of suggestions that can be explored in classrooms on a tentative basis. Personality theories are good for stimulating creative thought in education; no profession is in greater need of it.

The human personality is not a product of any narrow set of determinants. The influences that bear upon it can hardly be reduced to simple formulas based solely upon the deterministic assumption or upon the notion of autonomy. Psychologists have much to learn about personality before they are ready to give educators sound advice about how schools can improve affective development. When the school attempts to reshape personalities influenced by forces in conflict with the values held by teachers and school administrators, the results are likely to be abortive. Perhaps some short-term effects may be accomplished, but the negative effects may be greater than the positive.

One alternative that has been introduced to avoid this failure is to take the child as he is and to encourage his development along lines in harmony with his background. The effort is not to reshape his personality but simply to help it grow in the direction in which it is already pointed. This technique is permissiveness. If the child is not inclined to read or to deal with mathematics problems, he should not be influenced to do so. The main purpose is to help him be a happy and well-functioning member of his subculture. But permissiveness can backfire when it serves to sustain a lack of skills that the child will need as he matures. It is not always easy to teach reading to an adolescent after a decade of neglect of such teaching. The handicap may be permanent because he may not overcome the gap between himself and others who have received years of early practice.

Effective education in personality development probably requires a high degree of social consensus about values and aims, a strong prevailing moral code, and schools equipped to further rather than change the basic personality traits inculcated by the larger society. When the school is expected to educate the child in the absence of such conditions, failure is almost inevitable.

The message so far boils down to the principle that conflicts in society will be reflected by conflicts in education and that schooling alone cannot resolve those conflicts. In general, the problems that education is expected to solve far exceed the capacity of the schools. If we examine just what the schools of today *are* equipped to do, it pretty much amounts to the teaching of a limited number of physical and mental skills. Teacher trainees take courses in the sciences, literature, the arts, and the humanities. They take special courses in how to teach reading, spelling, mathematics, and so on. They receive a limited amount of classroom contact under a supervisory teacher and learn about classroom management. They take, on the average, one course in psychology and one or two courses in educational psychology. Some of them learn about the problems and treatment of retarded students or other kinds of handicapped children, or about the problems of students from disadvantaged backgrounds. The bulk of their education, then, is in subject matter and in methods of teaching it. They are usually quite effective in helping students learn information and the basic skills necessary for further learning. But their effectiveness depends primarily upon the student. If the student is willing to learn, if he has average or above average certain aptitudes, and if his parents and friends support his educational efforts, then the teacher is a valuable person for helping the student succeed. But teachers should not be expected to correct all the disadvantages imposed upon a child by his upbringing or by the negative influences of gangs, cliques, or community (such as fear or a sense of self-doubt). It is unrealistic to expect a teacher to deal effectively with problems outside the realm of his training.

Many innovations have been tried in education, but none has really succeeded that required skills extending beyond the limits of the teacher's basic expertise—the teaching of certain physical and mental arts. Even expert psychologists often fail to help their patients overcome problems that teachers are expected to handle while dealing with a host of other problems. The teacher is not a magician, but somehow the public has a hard time accepting that fact. Indeed, the public displays both unrealistic and paradoxical attitudes toward education. On the one hand, it has a naive faith that somehow education can take care of virtually all problems. But on the other hand, it is quick to criticize, to offer advice, and to make sweeping prescriptions for teachers. Faith in instructional methods and in the teacher's ability to deal with routine tasks is often quite scant, but faith in the overall process called "education" is almost limitless. The two attitudes are incompatible. One of the best things that could happen for education is a change in the public attitude toward it. If that attitude were to become more realistic, it is plausible to think that the public would begin to distribute responsibilities for total human development in a more sensible fashion. The current excessive expectancies of what the school can produce have led to spiraling school budgets along with decreasing effectiveness, particularly in areas that are not compatible with the teacher's professional training. The beefed-up budgets have, in effect, changed schools into bulky bureaucracies, especially in metropolitan regions. Many special departments exist that have no direct relation to student achievement. Such programs have not been properly evaluated, but it is reasonable to suspect that their cost exceeds the value of services produced. It might be profitable to subject them to critical assessment and to discontinue them if their productivity is poor or questionable. Such de-bureaucratization is not only likely to lower the cost of education but it might also improve teaching effectiveness by simplifying the task of accountability. When a bureaucracy is huge and bulky, it is hard to pinpoint responsibility.

Students are quite flexible and they are capable of learning many skills. But the habits, attitudes, and values, that students acquire before attending school and in situations external to school cannot be magically reshaped by teachers. Nearly every child, however, has the potential to think. And as he approaches adolescence his capacity to think in abstract terms becomes ripe for development. If we fail to tap his power to analyze, to apply his ideas to real situations, and to create plausible alternatives, his personal freedom will be pretty much limited to the passive and Skinnerian forms. Creative freedom is a correlate of thought, and the more people tend to flee from thinking, to seek substitutes for it, and to become creatures of habit and feeling, the more vulnerable they are to external pressures; in short, the more they fit the deterministic mold.

The teacher has almost unlimited opportunities to stimulate analysis, to help students become adept in identifying the elements of complex situations. The tools of analysis are found in logic and in the various principles of science. For example, ecology can be taught so that students are able to examine novel situations and to identify many of the positive and negative elements that bear upon the welfare of living things. The ability to perform reasonable analyses of that sort tends to free the individual from the influence of schemes designed to exploit ignorance. And this ability is the first step in creating promising alternatives. Without adequate knowledge and the ability to analyze plus skill in creating choices, a person cannot be an effective contributor in the democratic process.

ART, EDUCATION, AND FREEDOM

The main connection between education and freedom is found not in science but in art. The essence of art is skill. It is unfortunate that popular usage confines art to such activities as painting, sculpture, music, and poetry. Art is really broader than that. Let us regard it, therefore, as any pattern of skill that is used in an effort to achieve a maximum effect. Most art is not perfect, but all good art approaches or nearly reaches a point of optimal effect. If we adopt this broad notion of art instead of the more popular but narrow meaning, we can connect art with education in a most significant way. In the first place, our broad concept of art can be divided into several special fields. The *useful arts,* such as bricklaying and cooking, require skill in manipulating physical things that can be used and consumed. The *cooperative arts,* such as gardening, conservation, medicine, teaching, and counseling, employ skills in cooperation with certain natural tendencies. The gardener cooperates with the proclivities of a plant by supplying it with optimal conditions for growth. The physician uses his knowledge about natural defenses against disease to abet them rather than to supersede them. Teaching is a cooperative art, because the teacher cannot mold the child as the potter molds clay. The child has a natural tendency to learn, and the role of the teacher is to comprehend and cooperate with that tendency. Such cooperation is expressed when the student and teacher interact so that their mutual efforts combine to promote progress toward certain ends. Contrariwise, when the teacher selects tasks that are beyond the child's readiness and which presents them in a manner that runs counter to the basic principles of learning, the outcome will be negative. Teaching is rooted in communication, which depends upon the use of certain cooperative skills. The *competitive arts* are most common in sports, where skill vies with skill. Boxing, football, baseball, track, golf, and the like are contests to determine which person or team can outperform the opposition. Although team sports require cooperation, their main objective is a competitive one. The *liberal arts* are identified by an ancient distinction between manual and purely mental activity. Mathematics, logic, philosophy, and linguistics are good examples of the liberal arts. They play an important role in the analysis of conditions, interpretation of information, and creation of new alternatives and provocative problems. They provide much of the substance for the exercise of cognitive freedom. The *aesthetic arts,* such as music, poetry, dancing, painting, and sculpture, are involved with the creation of compositions that are ends in themselves. The aesthetic arts seem to emerge in a culture only after some development of the utilitarian arts.

When we recognize the range of activities comprehended by the useful, cooperative, competitive, liberal, and aesthetic arts, we see that most if not all of education is concerned with art. Indeed, one could arguably consider education as that enterprise which attempts to promote art. Even science fits into this broad conception of art because its functional aspects are included within the skills that make up the various arts. The liberal arts, for example, are fundamental to the analyzing of data, the making of logical interpretations, the creation of hypotheses, and the building of theories. The useful arts are needed to translate the concepts of science into concrete products. The cooperative arts, particularly education, are important for making science function as a public enterprise. The aesthetic arts are often a source of inspiration to scientists. Science, in turn, influences the aesthetic arts by creating new devices for producing sounds, by supplying new media for painters and sculptors, and by producing new ideas that can find dramatic expression through the fine arts.

The infant is unskilled, artless; his humanness has yet to reach fruition through growth and learning. A person who is hopelessly brain-damaged and survives only at the vegetable level is not endowed with the same degree of humanness that marks a mature and well-balanced adult. Humanness is a matter of degree and is essentially a growth function. It depends upon the acquisition of a variety of skills. The learning of art, the process of education, and becoming human are wrapped in the same developmental package. Education is optimal when it results in balanced development, when one achieves a good measure of the useful, cooperative, competitive, liberal, and aesthetic arts. The freedom of Skinner lacks scope. It is clear-cut and important, but it fails to embrace the full range of freedom that is found in art.

Education can promote the learning of arts because the arts are composed of skills that can be demonstrated and reduced to rather clear patterns of doing. Coaching supported by the adroit use of differential reinforcement can go far in the teaching of concrete skills. But because teaching is a cooperative art, it cannot have much effect unless the student has the readiness and desire to enter the cooperative process. That readiness is a product of early nurture and maturation. If a child's early training is not compatible with the direction in which education is prepared to move him, his educational growth will be stunted.

Effective teaching is not simply a set of techniques for producing change. It is much more than that. The techniques of teaching are always meshed into a larger framework, one that includes values, direction, and a guiding belief system. The techniques are effective only within the broader perspective.

Each type of art represents freedom. To some degree, proficiency in any of the arts can yield economic and/or social freedom. An unskilled electrician, for example, cannot compete on the job market with a journeyman. He is unfree or limited in exchanging what skill he may have in electrical work for economic gain. Social freedom or the ability to engage in satisfying interaction with others results from learning a set of skills associated with the cooperative arts. The competitive arts often break down certain barriers to the enjoyment of freedom. For example, standout Black athletes usually enjoy more freedom than many others in their ethnic group because of the recognition given to their competitive skills. Masters of the aesthetic arts also acquire similar freedoms, largely in the economic and social spheres.

But the special freedom that each art provides is the skill to deal with particular classes of problems. While the useful, cooperative, competitive, and aesthetic arts provide certain freedoms, they are all limited in comparison with the liberal arts. The scope of freedom offered by the latter is large. The cognitive skills of logical analysis and evaluation imported in the liberal arts equip one so trained to spot shoddy thinking, weak statements, logical fallacies, and untestable claims whether they occur in politics, education, art criticism, or any field, without regard to any particular "speciality." Although experts in the liberal arts remain vulnerable to nostrums, fads, and fallacies, they are less likely to accept them than those who lack their skills.

The liberal arts should not be confused with political liberalism. Efforts to equate the two spring from either ignorance or propaganda. Some self-styled literati or intelligentsia are prone to set fads and fashions with the implication that those who resist them cannot be accepted within the select circle of worthwhile thinkers. Some publications appear to set such fashions. Thus, the very cognitive freedom that is expressed by intellectual skills tends to be subverted by cliques that are usually notable for their lack of creative contributions. The term "intellectual fashion" is self-contradictory, since fashion tends to act as a substitute for thought. A kind of snob appeal emerges based on intellectual fashion, allowing the pseudointellectual entrance via magazine subscription into a sterile circle of mutual admirers. The current fashion of equating intellectualism and liberalism is a political ploy used by those who are more interested in power than in productive thought.

No ideology can capture and hold the field of analytical and creative thinking. There are no boundaries to cognitive freedom, and no party line or fashion can limit its expression in those who have the ability and desire to think. Education can provide opportunities and stimulation for cognitive growth. It can also inhibit thought by imposing fashionable "isms," presented as the gateway to enlightenment. But once a person has experienced the freedom provided by creative reflection, he is not likely to be intimidated by intellectual fads. To the extent that higher education is politicized, the conditions for independence of thought are curtailed. Whether such control is exercised by the right or the left makes little difference.

In summary, the freedom offered by education is found in the arts. Skills that make up the arts can be learned and they can broaden the scope of effective action. Severe lack of skills in communication, in social interaction, in dealing with the physical environment, and in manipulating ideas imposes the kinds of limitations and constraints that are incompatible with freedom. Finally, humanness cannot reach its full growth unless the most distinctive potential of the human, namely, cognitive freedom, is developed.

ACADEMIC FREEDOM

When a teacher or professor defines academic freedom it is usually in terms of his right to say whatever he feels is important in the course of carrying out his professional duties. He holds that free selection of materials, unrestricted writing and publication, and absence of pressure by means of official sanctions to mold the curriculum are essential parts of academic freedom. Such freedom is deemed necessary to education on the grounds that reliable and useful information cannot conform completely to any preset biases. Education provides the kind of learning that serves as the foundation for innovations, and if education is limited by political rules for the convenience of an elite, it cannot function in the best interest of all.

This rationale for academic freedom makes a great deal of sense. The extent to which academic freedom is limited may be a good index of the educational ineffectiveness of an institution. It may seem that any attack on such freedom must amount to support of totalitarian control. Unfortunately, the problem is not so simple. When we see that the roots of freedom are anchored more in speculation than in the world of facts, we see that it is not defensible to make categorical conclusions about its absolute goodness. Reality does not cater to the preconceptions of people despite some philosophical arguments to the contrary. So it seems that we must fall back on the old pragmatic criterion of making judgments about academic freedom according to the consequences that it produces.

To demonstrate the significance of the pragmatic criterion, we may begin with this question: under what conditions would academic freedom yield negative results? I can, of course, provide only a hypothetical answer. But I think that the answer is sufficiently plausible to give cause to doubt the absolute goodness of academic freedom under any and all circumstances.

Let us assume the existence of the following conditions in a given college classroom: (1) The professor knows more about the subject matter than his students. (2) The students acknowledge that the professor knows more about the material than they do. (3) The professor has a crusading spirit. (4) He does not limit his lectures to facts. (5) He is most interested in getting students to accept his theories and general belief pattern. (6) He wants to stimulate his students to action, to take what they learn and translate it into reality. (7) He has an engaging personality. (8) He is an effective speaker and has a touch of charisma. (9) His students are impressionable; they are looking for something exciting and different. (10) His students are not well trained in the skills of cognitive freedom, particularly in critical analysis and evaluation. These ten conditions are not unrealistic. They probably obtain in thousands of classrooms across the country.

We now assume that our hypothetical professor operates in a situation of maximum academic freedom. It would seem that one likely outcome is effective indoctrination, that is, the uncritical acceptance by the students of some mixture of facts and speculation. It is unlikely that the speculative or theoretical parts of the professor's message are entirely free from error, questionable assumptions, unfounded bias, and conclusions that do not accord with reality. The question now arises: what about the academic freedom of students? Has it been adroitly swept under the rug or camouflaged so that it becomes confused with indoctrination? Has it been manipulated out of existence?

The defenders of academic freedom will rightly respond that although this freedom may sometimes be abused, as the above situation suggests, the illustration provides no basis for abandoning the freedom. Of course, their reply is sound.

But it does not suggest how the negative aspects of academic freedom can be minimized. Let me attempt an answer to this problem.

The unfortunate effects on students of the actions of our hypothetical instructor can be reasonably held in check if the school administration establishes the following policies: (1) Select a balanced faculty. The biases of one faculty member should be offset by equally plausible biases in other members. This means a highly homogeneous faculty, particularly with respect to political ideology, should not occur. (2) Saturate the curriculum with the teaching of cognitive skills. No student could escape being exposed to the skills of sound criticism, evaluation, identification of basic assumptions, discrimination between fact and opinion, identification of testable assertions, development of plausible problems, hypothesis-making, and the like. (3) Provide special recognition or reward for students who show evidence of development of cognitive skills, independent judgment, and creative solutions to problems.

Unless these suggestions or equivalent ones are adopted, the student does not stand a good chance of developing the kind of independence that education should provide. The suggested program does not rule out the possibility of attempts by professors to indoctrinate. The goal of eliminating indoctrination is not realistic. Indeed, it may not even be a desirable aim because the growth of student academic freedom, which is deemed the same as cognitive freedom, can probably not occur unless the student is exposed to conflicting arguments, efforts at persuasion, and the personal magnetism of instructors. Only in the intellectual cafeteria of diverse offerings can students grow in the acquisition of cognitive skills. It is a kind of growth that will serve them well in many situations beyond the confines of the school. The important point we are making is that faculty freedom does not by itself necessarily guarantee the development of cognitive freedom in students.

When we look at the conditions in our universities and colleges, can we find substantial hope for the development of academic (cognitive) freedom in students? I do not have sufficient information to answer this question accurately. Yet it seems clear that higher education is not pointed in the direction of maximizing those skills on which such freedom depends. Department members of a typical faculty of sociologists, for example, appear too homogeneous in attitudes, beliefs, and the like. Hence, the indoctrination is too one-sided, and the student is left with the feeling that he has been emancipated from a set of shackling beliefs while in reality he has probably only exchanged one set of biases for another. The subtle aspect of such indoctrination leads the student to believe that he has truly gained enlightenment and freedom in the process of being captured by the ideas of someone else, without exercising the critical reflection that can be his only safeguard to personal freedom. The picture looks bleak, but it may contain some basis for hope.

The conditions which I have suggested for ensuring academic freedom of the student are not easy to meet. And it is unlikely that they can or will be met. For example, the selection of a balanced faculty, particularly in a single department, appears nearly impossible to realize. The most feasible part of my program is the inclusion of cognitive training in many parts of the curriculum. I would settle for that, with the hope that most students would be motivated to develop those skills that can give them a sense of personal independence in the realm of ideas.

CHAPTER 8

Survival of Cognitive Freedom and Other Futuristic Estimates

I have judged Skinnerian freedom as a concept useful in describing one form of freedom, but not broad enough to cover all the nonfictitious meanings. My claim is that the assumption of determinism is valuable to a limited extent. It cannot be used, however, as handily as can the assumption of free choice in dealing with the behavior of productive thought. Since both assumptions are speculations and since no final decision can be made in favor of one over the other, it seems best, as a general conclusion, to admit both. Each one has a particular strength and usefulness relative to the nature of the task in which one engages. Some purposes autonomatically lend themselves to the assumption of determinism, such as most scientific work. But other behavior makes sense only if one assumes freedom.

Cognitive freedom is the achievement of personal independence involving such processes as evaluation, analysis, and hypothesis making. Unless a person has some proficiency in cognitive skills he has no defense against artful efforts to exploit his gullibility. He remains an unthinking "party-liner" who behaves according to the deterministic formula, his reactions being turned on or off by the external situation as if he were a machine. When a person fails to achieve some proficiency in the cognitive skills, then, his personal freedom is largely an illusion. But if he can suspend his judgment until he has made an adequate assessment, his conclusion is likely to be quite different from one based on impulse. The main weakness of impulse as a guide to freedom lies in the fact that rewards can be manipulated to stimulate an impulse that will lead to entrapment. Cognitive freedom necessarily involves the process of looking ahead, of examining the situation carefully and mentally testing a variety of possible decisions to estimate what is likely to ensue from each. It is often impossible to predict the results of deliberation. It is also impossible to describe deliberation in causal terms without engaging in questionable speculation that has no more substance than is contained in the assumption of freedom. It seems, therefore, that there is a significant advantage in switching frequently between the freedom and determinism assumptions according to convenience, simplicity, and utility. It is too awkward, tiresome, and impractical to cling rigidly to one assumption over the other in any and all situations. The indeterminate nature of the free will–determinism issue suggests that a relative, pragmatic stance is more workable than the less flexible kinds of mental orientation.

My suggestions for making education more freedom-producing resemble John Dewey's platform. He saw in reflective thinking or problem solving the key to educational growth, as described in his book *How We Think*. My analysis simply attempts to provide some psychological considerations that broaden the support for his thesis.

After all my assessments, judgments, and suggestions have been made, the question remains: so what? Is my platform more feasible than Skinner's? This is the crucial question. So it is time to take a critical look at the workability of the things advocated here. I cannot deny that my program of action seems more desirable than Skinner's. But desirability and feasibility are quite different. To achieve cognitive freedom one should practice critical evaluation of his own pet notions.

CONDITIONS THAT INHIBIT COGNITIVE FREEDOM

When I examine my suggestions in the light of social reality, I am depressed by discovering conditions that make my hopes and program somewhat improbable of realization. The following features of our social environment seem to me to inhibit the expression of cognitive freedom.

ABUNDANCE OF ALTERNATIVES THAT PROMISE IMMEDIATE GRATIFICATION

Our technology has produced a great variety of ways to indulge ourselves without much effort. We have almost countless ways to tickle our senses: movies, television and radio, amusing books, and so on. And with the demise of Puritanism has come a legitimization of self-indulgence. Sensual pleasures are easy to come by, and the temptation they offer is hard to resist. This Disneyland of variety and the production of instant pleasure tend to camouflage the need for reflective thought. Why should a person stay home and read a history book when so many alternatives are available to amuse him without any effort? The fun culture is not the kind of environment that makes reflection very inviting.

STIMULUS PROFUSION

Technology as it has been applied has created a "busy" environment. We live in a world filled with attention-getting devices. The stimulus level is high and considerably varied. Billboards, TV and radio commercials, showy displays of all sorts, particularly in the field of fads and fashions, slick-magazine articles, the ebb and flow of traffic controlled by demanding signals of stop, go, and caution—all these comprise only a tiny sample of the profusion of stimuli. During a typical day, the average urban citizen experiences a kaleidoscope of many urges, most of which he is unable to satisfy because of insufficient time to consummate them and because of the canceling effect produced by other stimuli. These urges are conceived and aborted with considerable speed. To stimulate an urge and then inhibit its expression probably increases the general level of inner tension. And in the main, stimulus profusion tends to keep attention span at a low level. Reflection, however, often requires sustained attention over a considerable time span. But in an environment of stimulus profusion any effective progress on problem solving must be scheduled on a time-sharing basis; that is, short spurts of concentration are spread out over some time period. Even the traditional image of the professor's life has changed. He cannot use his office as a place for thinking and creative activities. He must find some retreat in the library stacks or in the basement of his home to get enough time for productive concentration. If he is among the elite in his profession he may be lucky enough to visit a "think tank," where he can devote all the time he wishes to concentrated effort. It has not been established that creative work is best done in short spurts. In fact, the evidence suggests the contrary, that productive people typically must enjoy prolonged retreats in which they are sealed off from the busyness of the outside world.

POLITICAL POLARIZATION

During the sixties a noticeable increase occurred in political involvement and activism. Many factions sprouted to launch crusades against some aspect of the establishment. No one would deny that the status quo could stand considerable improvement. But the style used in promoting change is important. If the style is noisy, emotional, and pregnant with violence, the reaction will be noisy, emotional, and violent. It was hard to discern any rational grounds for some of the violence spawned in the crusade for change. The establishment reacted as expected. It legitimized some of the new departures, while mobilizing force against those factions with which it could not compromise. The general consequence has been that most of the crusading factions have become tired and have curtailed their direct action. But the pot still simmers, and no one is sure just what to expect.

The climate that polarization creates is not conducive to thoughtful analysis or productive thought of high quality. Although polarization tends to sharpen differences and so, in one sense, clarify issues, the psychological effect is largely emotional; political polarization adds to the noisiness of the environment and encourages impulsive action rather than deliberation. Effective communication becomes difficult because people find it hard to take the time and effort to hear just what the opposition is saying. While the crusaders for change continually accuse the establishment of not listening, the failure to listen is shared by both sides. In fact, it seems that the crusaders assume that it is unnecessary to listen to their opponents because they know the position of the opposition only too well. The crusaders, therefore, often prove to be poorer listeners than members of the establishment. They sometimes appear to be more rigid and less likely to make practical compromises. But this judgment is a superficial one and cannot be applied to all of the factions that advocate change.

INCREASED UNPOPULARITY OF RATIONAL ACTIVITIES

We are told that enrollment in science courses has steadily decreased. A growing number of young people adopt an antiscience attitude and see technology as the tool of exploiters. They see little reason to devote their lives to the growth of science and technology when these fields have produced the conditions which threaten to rob the person of his humanistic qualities. The image of science is currently not a flattering one. Its seamy sides have been emphasized and its positive aspects minimized. Science, regarded as the domain of reason, reflection, logical problem solving, and the like, is also charged with having given rise to the growth of antihumanitarian forces. So the very seat of rational problem solving has acquired a negative image.

INCREASED POPULATION

The mere production of more and more people is not, in itself, a significant factor militating against reflection. But the conditions in which it occurs tend to make it one of the contributing factors. The simple limitation of living space produced by increased population seems to increase tension. When stimulus profusion rises in a polarized environment that encourages irrationality, the individual faces increased noise, and perhaps an increased tendency to impulsiveness, as he is crowded by increasing numbers of his fellows.

FRACTIONATION OF THE SOCIAL VALUE SYSTEM

When a society has a common core of beliefs that functions to influence daily life, people pretty much know what to expect from one another. Shared values form a part of the cement that holds the society together. When that cement crumbles, many different value systems emerge.

Some of them are mutually incompatible, and the respective believers form groups which view each other with estrangement. The hippie, for example, is eyed with suspicion by others, to whom his beliefs appear threatening. He therefore tends to associate only with his own kind, because his source of support and approval is limited to those who share his values. The same tendency can be seen in many other people who constitute clear-cut subcultures, such as motorcycle gangs, middle-class swingers, intellectual liberals, educated conservatives, members of the drug culture, and so on. Fractionation of the core values lends fuel to the political polarization tendency. It seems as though each value system attracts an island of adherents, who see other islands as unfriendly or hostile, and limit their communication with those islands to the necessary exchange of goods, money, and services. Little if any spare time is devoted to serious and mutually respectful interchange across the islands.

Before one can engage in useful thinking he must hold some set of values and beliefs. But in a polarized environment, when thinkers in one subculture come up with ideas of plausibility and worth, little recognition is given them by other groups. Even when productive ideas are distributed by the mass media, members of different islands are unlikely to assess them adequately. For example, Skinner's book *Beyond Freedom and Dignity* has received mostly negative reactions because Skinner is judged as belonging to a certain class, namely, that of cold-blooded technologists who wish to destroy democracy and control society by a conditioning system based on scientific principles bereft of humanitarian values. It seems difficult if not impossible even for many educated persons to break through that mental set about Skinner and exercise the kind of cognitive freedom that his message merits. The fractionation of values provides an atmosphere in which productive thinking may have a small audience.

LACK OF TRAINING IN THE DISCIPLINE OF THINKING

Although Dewey made a most appealing and logical case for using the schools to promote reflection, efforts to implement his suggestions have largely failed. Such efforts could not compete with the many alternatives that promised instant gratification. The school was forced to legitimize activities that militated against the growth of reflective thought. Although amusement and recreation are not inherently bad, proliferation of such activities is not conducive to a climate of reflection, unless the management of conditions is quite skillful.

Skinner is probably correct about the power of reinforcement. The rewards offered by a variety of activities that require no long delay before gratification are most appealing. Productive thought, however, usually imposes the constraint of a delayed reward. Frustration tolerance must be reasonably high. But when technology has been applied to the creation of means for instant gratification and those means become a part of the nurturing process, it is unlikely that the kind of frustration tolerance that makes reflective thought attractive will be developed. Skinner is calling for a new way of managing the environment so that frustration tolerance and other desirable habits can be effectively conditioned. But his suggestions are largely rejected because his evaluation of the human being appears unflattering.

It seems unlikely that the schools will be able to create conditions that will motivate students to develop the skills necessary for the expression of cognitive freedom. The mental set of both students and teachers is currently not hospitable to the discipline of rational reflection. Meanwhile, the problems that demand deliberate thought for their solution are becoming increasingly critical. The whole matrix of conditions suggests that any effective solution to our problems is not going to be achieved within the democratic process.

Before democracy can be effective, each participant must be able to assess, judge, and make plausible contributions. These activities cannot be divorced from rational thought. The disciplines required for effective problem solving are not popular and the social system is not ready to support the kind of school training necessary to promote acquisition of skills in those disciplines. If Dewey is correct in thinking that the schools merely reflect the predominant forces of society, it seems hopeless to expect that skills not supported by society will be taught effectively.

The upshot of this discouraging analysis is that Skinner probably offers one of the few realistic solutions. The conditions discussed above respecting our attitude towards problem-solving can only reinforce the Skinnerian analysis.

ECOLOGY AND FREEDOM

Skinner says that the environment acts as a selective mechanism. It determines what behavior is necessary for survival and what behavior will lead to death or extinction. One cannot, for example, jump from a high cliff onto jagged rocks below and expect to remain unharmed. One cannot eat or drink poisonous substances and expect no bad results. Examples can be easily multiplied to show that one's welfare is dependent on how he interacts with the environment. Effective learning depends upon environmental feedback. The learner does something, performs some act, which produces certain consequences. If the consequences are harmful or unpleasant, the learner is not likely to repeat the act. But if the results are pleasant (reinforcing) and seen as beneficial, the act will be repeated, and its frequency will rise until it tends to become a habit. Behavior is formed, therefore, according to the experienced results of one's own efforts. But some things that we do cannot be so easily evaluated. We do not always know just what consequences will be produced, because they may be delayed and not easily perceived as connected with some particular act. When one contributes to environmental pollution, for example, he usually experiences no direct aversive consequences. In fact, he may experience positive consequences and will therefore tend to repeat the act. But when millions of people engage in the same pollution-producing act, the damage to the environment adds up. Eventually, the environment may become unfit for habitation.

Many ecologists warn us that we cannot increase the gross national product as population continues to rise without disastrous consequences. Despite such warnings, there seem to be only token efforts to check pollution and population growth. Skinner's psychology provides a good explanation of why we find ourselves in this difficult situation and why it is going to be so hard to do anything about it in time to avert a global disaster. In the first place, modern technology has been applied to provide many creature comforts. By earning money, people buy these comforts. They are made and sold as quickly as the means for production and sale can be arranged. Habits of consumption create a demand for more goods and services, particularly as population rises. It is rewarding or reinforcing to buy and consume things. The immediate consequences are pleasing. The long-range consequences, however, appear to be threatening. Skinner tells us that our behavior is most strongly influenced by the *immediate* consequences that it produces. For example, we see an attractive ad for snowmobiles. Repetition of the ad tends to have an effect on us by a kind of Pavlovian conditioning. We earn extra money and purchase a snowmobile. The act of buying is itself reinforcing because it brings the expectation of enjoying the product into the realm of immediate possibility. Affluent shoppers, therefore, are prone to buy many things that they do not really need. Shopping is fun. It is rewarding in and of itself. Many things that are bought remain unused; yet, new things continue to be bought, and become allotted to junk piles. This suggests that the habit of overbuying can easily become very strong. Excessive buying supports expansion of the GNP, a good index of pollution growth.

When ecologists warn us that our habits of buying create environmental dangers, we are put in a conflict situation. We don't want to give up habits that have become so pleasant. We perceive little in the way of direct negative effect of our habits, but we experience quite a bit of immediate satisfaction. The competition between immediate satisfaction and delayed aversive consequences is an unequal contest. By nature, according to Skinner, we succumb to the immediate gratifiers and avoid the bad results that we produce. The junk piles we generate are quickly taken from our sight by a regular removal service. That is negative reinforcement, which merely strengthens our habit of cooperating with the garbage collectors. Getting the refuse out of sight quickly removes us from the aversive effect that it produces. So we continue to overbuy and to help the people hired to get the junk out of sight with dispatch and efficiency. The immediate effect is comfortable and pleasing. We cannot see or measure just how much we contribute to pollution. It is easy for us, therefore, to rationalize our behavior and stick with the pleasant habits that we have learned. The cycle becomes almost impossible to break. There is little hope that the problem will be solved by voluntary efforts. The only alternative that is open for dealing with the problem effectively seems to be some type of systematic control.

The democratic legislative process may not achieve the needed results, because the pressure put upon legislators is likely to reflect the strength of habits that have been established by consumptive rewards. It seems, therefore, that democracy is inherently unable to deal with environmental problems until they have reached the crisis stage.

Democratic societies can usually mobilize their efforts effectively in dealing with an immediate threat, such as imminent war. They exhibit an unusual ability to sacrifice immediate gratification to avoid military defeat. But the threat must be strong and clearly perceived. The warnings issued by ecologists, however, often appear remote, and many people interpret them as scare tactics to divert attention from more important social ills and to excuse ourselves from dealing with those ills. Our people become divided and no effective cooperation is forthcoming. Not until a crisis stage is reached is it likely that we shall be able to congeal our efforts. It may then be too late to avert wholesale suffering and involuntary population pruning.

The ecological threats may be exaggerated, as some experts assert. Yet the continued warnings of environmental disaster and the various counter-claims produce an atmosphere of anxiety that may weaken the effectiveness of democratic leadership. But perhaps the main threat to the health of our democracy lies in that combination of conditions that makes rational activities unpopular. A democracy of infants is a self-contradictory concept.

Some readers may object to the interpretation that our psychological climate is becoming increasingly hostile to the democratic process. They may reject my claim on the grounds that at no other time in our history have people, especially young people, shown so much interest in politics. Young people are entering the political area in large numbers, and their zeal and dedication more than offset their lack of experience. In general, they exhibit strong humanistic ideals and they are bent on translating those ideals into reality. Therefore, some would say, it is not correct to say that our democracy is dying, that it cannot survive the current crisis.

I would very much like to accept that position, because it is comforting and hopeful. Unfortunately, the facts that it is based on appear insufficient. For example, there is no logical connection between increased interest in politics and democracy. Also, idealism that is uncompromising tends to be antithetical to democratic processes. One can proclaim ideals and still be a totalitarian. Hitler is a good case in point. He stimulated an idealistic movement that brooked no compromise, all in the name of improving the quality of the human race. Dedicated idealists blessed with great energy are often not tempermentally attuned to the democratic process because they are already convinced that their aims are correct and should be adopted without modification. They tend to be impatient and may look upon democratic action as a slow and diluting process, which threatens the purity of their platform. So if they happen to get control of an important function they may go through the motions of democratic procedures while using whatever means they have to minimize the uncertainties that the democratic process entails.

Perhaps the key to the solution of the question of whether or not the psychological climate is becoming less hospitable to democracy rests in a comparison of the kinds of characteristics needed for democratic action with those personality features of the new political activists. There seems to be little doubt that no effective democracy can exist unless those engaged in the political process, especially leaders, have the capacity to compromise. They cannot be too rigid because they must somehow get along with their adversaries. They must be attuned to pragmatic assessment, that is, the art of looking ahead and estimating the probable consequences of their decisions. These and allied characteristics seem to be necessary for any viable democratic process. I am not sure to what degree the young political activists have such traits. But according to observed samples of questionable merit, there is some doubt as to whether they do. The most fearsome quality of their behavior is a rigid dogmatism that appears to be unprepared for compromise. I hope that I am wrong. But it is difficult to be optimistic when it seems that conditions antithetical to critical and productive reflection, as discussed earlier, have dominated the upbringing of the new breed of politician.

SPECULATIONS ON THE FUTURE: A SCIENCE-FICTION LOOK

No one is sure of just what the future holds. Yet I cannot resist airing some thoughts about the future, because the effort may add some effect to the argument alleging a critical need to make the acquisition of rational skills more attractive. Admittedly, my methods are gross and quite uncertain. My speculations are of a quasi-science-fiction sort that uses a liberal amount of imagination to project trends to their logical extremes.

I suspect that the rise of labor unions during the late 1700s and early 1800s in America launched a trend that even today is not fully comprehended. New movements often begin with the best of intentions, and as they gain momentum, somewhere along the way they take on features that were not foreseen at the beginning. And some of these features introduce practices that threaten to defeat the entire movement. Unionism may be a case in point. It obviously became a powerful political force. Its success stimulated many different groups to unite and enter into collective bargaining so as to improve their economic status and power. We now have teacher unions and other organized groups that were deemed unlikely to arise even a few decades ago. But no single union is sufficiently powerful to dominate politics; there is no complete federation of all unions.

The rise of unionism has increased political sensitivity by demonstrating its influence on political leaders. That and the above remarks about unions are quite obvious. But few have

stopped to consider what could happen if a heretofore un-
organized group that develops and maintains the technical
power systems on which we depend suddenly became
united. I refer to scientists, engineers, and other technologists who create the means of power necessary to meet the
physical and other needs of the population. It is difficult to
overestimate the power that a brotherhood of scientists and
technologists could control. Their power would not be confined to striking, which is the main weapon of other unions.
On the contrary, the strike would probably not be used at
all. To get some insight into the many manifestations of
power that technicians and scientists hold in their grasp, let
us consider a realistic situation. Military leaders must depend upon an army of technicians to gather and analyze information necessary for making decisions. These leaders
would be helpless without their technical staffs. In effect, it
is quite likely that nearly all important decisions are actually
not made by military leaders, but by those who compile,
process, and analyze the huge amounts of data pertinent to
the operation. The colonel or general cannot possibly understand all the intricacies of the technical work upon which he
depends. Any given general could probably easily be eliminated from his post by an alliance of technicians who wish to
remove him. They could predispose him to write commands
that would lead to his early retirement. The process could be
a gradual one and the general could no nothing to stop it
because of his lack of skill in pinpointing the trouble. He is
not a technical analyst and he is pretty much at the mercy
of his technical advisors. The same relationship holds between top politicians and their technical staffs. If a union of
scientists and technicians wanted to dismiss a president, they
could perform the task more easily than any other group.

Let us assume that the trend in the spread of unionization
will eventually result in a union of technologists, and that
this alliance will hold to a set of values and beliefs that are

not in agreement with those of democracy. Furthermore, let us imagine that this group will regard the usual democratic leaders as both incompetent and potentially dangerous. Because its members will be the most able citizens in comprehending and manipulating the sources of scientifically produced power, it could pool its skills for the purpose of dominating the traditional leaders, who may be either eliminated or retained as puppets. This powerful union would comprise members dealing with the collection, analysis, and interpretation of technical data. It would include physicists, chemists, engineers, biologists, physicians, psychologists, economists, sociologists, electronic experts, and others. These groups would adopt a common credo that would essentially amount to the belief that current leaders in politics and industry were incapable of coping with the complexities that confront them. They would adopt a working platform of values and would regard themselves as the only ones capable of stopping the trend toward disaster. They would agree that their advice to current leaders is typically misunderstood and that decisions are adopted that run counter to what they deem as right and necessary. They would oppose current leadership and consider it their humanitarian duty to get rid of the dangerous elements in the system. If such a unity of purpose ever occurred among the groups named, no power could stop them. They could easily place elected leaders under their command while camouflaging all signs of the change. There would be no bloody revolution, only a subtle coup d'état that would hardly cause a ripple on the surface.

Their easy success could be a heady tonic and one that might be difficult to manage. The sudden realization that they command the power of the nation and that no serious opposition stands in their way might tempt them to protect their success with secrecy. This would result in a tightly knit society of mutually interdependent members. Such a society would probably find it necessary to introduce a mythology and set of rituals to sustain its unity. And as its expansion of knowledge through research continued, the masses would grow increasingly ignorant because the new elite would see no reason for sharing their knowledge with a public incapable of grasping it. Indeed, the current antiscience attitude would fit neatly into this package, and that attitude would be abetted by the elite. The democratic ritual of voting would be sustained to provide the masses with the comfort of a traditional illusion.

The elite would need a means of tapping the budding geniuses among the masses to revitalize its store of genes. That process, however, could easily be accomplished with such inconspicuousness that no problems would arise. As time passed and the new regime was firmly seated, its exploding sources of knowledge would tend to make it almost totally estranged from the masses. The ruling elite would gradually lose feelings of responsibility for the welfare of the masses, and decisions would be made indicating a less than human regard for them. At that juncture, population pruning would be carried out with a clear conscience, and whatever masses remain would survive only in order to maintain a strong gene reserve for the elite.

The above bit of fantasy may seem too flimsy even to consider. It does, however, have one feature of substance. We live in an age that has a growing dependence upon the processing of huge quantities of information. Much of technology is devoted to communication. The lifeblood of government organizations is information flow. Bureaus must take incoming data, along with their own self-made noise, and send them through a maze of channels before decisions are made. The politician becomes more and more dependent upon data reduction because he cannot possibly grasp technicalities in their raw state—for example, certain ecological observations cast in the languages of chemistry, physics, biology, and mathematics. He has little understanding of the logic of computers, but many of his decisions are determined by computer outputs.

Information comes from far and wide. It must be sorted, analyzed, and interpreted in lay language before the highest-paid "leaders" can agree with what has already been decided by their staffs of technologists. Sometimes, in the process of making technical data intelligible to top officials a valuable part of it is either lost or camouflaged because some of it resists clear-cut translation into simple English. It is becoming clear that many heads of large organizations, both public and private, are working at their levels of incompetence, to use Peter's terminology. In general, technology has thrust the traditional leader into an archaic status. The main excuse for retaining him is to pamper tradition. But as figureheads become increasingly incompetent because of growing complexities, they also become dangerous. They are overwhelmed by the fast tempo of information, much of which they cannot understand except on a superficial level. So their chance of committing costly blunders increases exponentially. They are made to appear important only through the expertise of dutiful technologists.

The reduction of leaders to figureheads is not a modern phenomenon; it has a long history. For example, in England it was necessary to reduce kings to figureheads because they became incompetent to lead the nation as the empire started to grow, making conditions too complex for them to handle. They were replaced by more competent decision makers, who had numerous able workers to give them the proper help. The king was reduced to an honest figurehead; that is, he was no longer disguised as the central decision maker. This fact should inspire us to study our modern leaders carefully. Have they really an adequate grasp of the problems that face them? Would a combination of cooperative specialists have a clearer understanding? What is the chance that a powerful lay leader will misuse his power because of a failure to interpret technical facts correctly? How effective is the communication between a lay leader and his advisors? Do top leaders really have the best advisors, or are the latter less than adequate? At what point along the chain of command in a power hierarchy does the lay official tend to become incompetent? Are the current "think-tank" experts providing leaders with sound policy research? How many technical languages such as mathematics, physics, chemistry, biology, economics, psychology, and the like should a top leader be conversant with in order to have an adequate grasp of complex situations? If decisions are best made by teams of knowledgeable specialists, how should such teams be chosen? These are only some of the important questions that plague those who suspect that an entirely new pattern of leadership must be established before decision making can appreciably increase in quality. The science fiction perspective given earlier implies that we can no longer sustain the illusion that our leaders are more than figureheads. But how valid is that perspective? We cannot even begin to approach answers to this and other equally important questions if we encourage the growth of irrational sentiments.

Our science fiction fantasy boldly implies that democracy has reached its limit of effectiveness. It has already broken down. And time used to patch it up is only wasted time. Hence, we must have the courage to face reality and must not only desire but demand that the decision-making process be put in better order. In clinging to traditional sentiments we necessarily move closer to catastrophe. So the only solution is to make an honest admission that democracy is outmoded and replace it with a more effective system, namely, a technical meritocracy.

How should we react to such a platform? First, we can afford to ignore it, if it is merely a baseless and imaginary threat. But that easy alternative may be dangerous, because many facts can be mustered and interpretations offered in support of the argument. So if it is a real threat, even if perhaps not an immediate one, we ought to consider how to meet it. I have no detailed plan. But it seems certain that one important change is to bring the general attitude toward cognitive skills into a more coherent and realistic focus. Both the advantages and limitations of these skills ought to be understood free of the fictions that typically entwine them. Rational reflection does not hold the answer to all problems. It should not be deemed so important that all nonrational experiences are downgraded or suppressed. But neither should it be maligned, ridiculed, or ignored, because such practices may force it underground, where it may be nurtured for vindictive purposes.

It has been said that Martin Luther longed for promotion within the Catholic hierarchy, and that when he was frustrated by the high command he turned his hurt feelings into the production of an attack that permanently crippled the jurisdiction of Catholicism. Whether this story is correct with respect to his motivation or not is beside the point; it is believable and psychologically plausible. Its moral is that it can be dangerous to hurt the pride of people with strong aptitudes and high energy. The current attitude toward scientists and technologists may create the spark to stimulate their unity and reaction. The scientific community is increasingly cast in an unfavorable light. This atmosphere gives scientists an uneasy feeling. They have been put on the defensive by an intellectual faddism. They are not very thick-skinned, and the negative stimulation is not easy to tolerate. They are looking for an out. Some of them are trying to make a compromise by humanizing the canons of scientific behavior. But that effort can go only so far. They are not likely to accept permanently the feelings of guilt and anxiety that have been foisted upon them. And they cannot help but notice the foibles of their critics. When all this fermentation jells into the realization that their collective force is irresistible, they will opt for power and gladly shed the humble garb that they have been forced to wear. To the extent that their egos have been wounded, they will find it convenient and rewarding to exercise some form of reprisal. Democracy may die without a whimper. The democratic rituals of primaries and elections are likely to continue, and much ado will be made about what candidates should be elected. But the process will be merely a charade. Power will have shifted into other hands.

Whether the above speculation is feasible or not may be unimportant. The main point is that current conditions suggest that we are creating a great social divide with respect to the cognitive skills. Scientific knowledge is growing at an increasing rate, and those at the cutting edge of that growth compose a small minority. Even more important is the fact that less and less new knowledge is coming within the grasp of the majority. The schools cannot keep apace with the knowledge explosion, partly because of the current intellectual climate among many young people. At the same time, new sources of power are being created from within the advanced areas of science and technology. For example, the biological sciences seem to be at the threshold of fantastic methods of control over organic processes, promising such possibilities as "cloning"—making carbon copies of any person in any given number—and the shaping of new genetic structures that could create a higher species of man. As the masses and traditional leaders become more and more removed from this new world of man-made realities, communication between the cognitive elite and the masses is likely to dwindle proportionately. And as that communication grows weaker the estrangement between the two spheres may increase until little if any autonomy remains in the world of archaic knowledge, the netherworld of the masses. If that end is realized, there is no doubt where the concentration of power will lie.

A FINAL NOTE

The entire thesis boils down to a philosophy of education. It holds that the pessimism of science fiction, as outlined above, is not the only plausible perspective regarding the future. We still have a choice. Perhaps the most important decision that we must make is to effect a more equitable distribution of the knowledge and skills that serve as sources of power. When schools dilute their offerings to the point that most students remain ignorant of power-producing knowledge, it seems inevitable that two estranged worlds—one dominant over the other—will evolve. The curriculum, therefore, may hold the key to the future. If we can manage the learning process so that the most significant knowledge and skills can be grasped by at least half of the student population, we ought to be able to prevent the threat described above. Such a defensive maneuver may require a change in our concept of democracy, particularly that part pertaining to freedom.

The most likely alternatives available to us are limited to about three: the decision to strengthen and modify democracy, the Skinnerian route, and a technological meritocracy.

The chance that democracy can be saved is a long shot. But it is worth taking.

CHAPTER 9

Description and Appraisal of the Skinnerian Society

If a Skinnerian world or something close to it is likely to occur in the foreseeable future, it is worthwhile to estimate just how it may come about and to outline the kind of life that it promises to yield. The popular image of the Skinnerian society is badly distorted and should be corrected. The Skinnerian society is often equated with those envisioned by *1984* and *Brave New World*; both equations are incorrect. The kind of technological meritocracy described in the previous chapter tends to approximate the *1984* model. But the Skinner plan appears to yield quite different results. I shall try to identify some of the main characteristics of the operant society to establish a reasonable expectancy of what the future may hold. First, I shall speculate on why the operant plan has a chance of succeeding. Next, the moral implications of the psychology will be examined. These two preliminary tasks should yield the kind of relevant considerations that are useful for estimating important features of the operant social system.

The attractiveness of Skinner's position as a proposal for social change is twofold. First, the position not only spotlights the failure of current methods in dealing with major problems, but also explains why those methods may continue to fail. It holds that a change in methodology, in the way we go about trying to solve important problems, is necessary for survival. Second, it provides a formula for survival and for improvement of social conditions. Skinner promises hope, direction, active involvement, and practical results. We should not underestimate the psychological appeal of such a movement.

It may not take much added force to make the movement snowball to such prominence that all other plans would be swept aside. Yet the Skinnerian strategy is not to create a bandwagon powered by sheer emotion. Rather, the approach is divided into two phases: an effective broadcast of the doctrine and a gradual use of the techniques, applied piecemeal to important problems. When and if the second phase becomes clearly established, the harvest of reinforcement will be sufficient to make the plan a way of life. Also, the program is championed with great sincerity. The unmistakable sincerity that Skinner shows must be taken as another force in favor of the movement.

It is a mistake to think that Skinner seeks to follow the *Walden II* model in getting his system integrated into the larger society. There will be no master manipulator pulling strings behind the scenes. The whole operation will be open and aboveboard. Skinner recognizes that it is good strategy to demonstrate publicly how conditions can be managed so as to cope with sticky problems. Reasons why the operant plan will be carried on publicly instead of secretly will be given at various points in later parts of the discussion.

One important detail in the plan is to set up priorities,

that is, to determine a chain of problems in a proper order so as to yield the greatest effect early in the application phase. It would be most effective to begin with a significant problem that could be handled quickly, followed by a second success, and so on.

Professor James McConnell of the University of Michigan —a pro-Skinnerian of a modified sort—thinks that no major social change can be brought about unless two events happen in the following order: first, a change must occur in the way people perceive the world about them and the relationship they bear to it; second, some procedure must be put into motion to show that the new perspective supports a technique that produces more rewarding results than the traditional system. For example, when surgery was first introduced, it was regarded as an affront to God's Word. At that time, the interpretation of the Scriptures held that the human body was the temple of God and that it was sinful to cut into it, to remove any of its parts. But as the doctrine of modern science expanded its influence, its perceptions about the human being, including his physical makeup, his relationship to other creatures, and his shaky status within the larger scheme of things, became more widely adopted and the belief climate became less hostile to the notion of surgery. But the wholesale adoption of surgery was not established merely by acceptance of the scientific perspective. It remained to be proved that surgery could be used to prolong life and to promote health. So within the new attitudinal context, the many demonstrations of surgical success finally overpowered the opposition. And today the whole moral tone about surgery is completely reversed in relation to its initial moral assessment. It would now be considered immoral for a surgeon to refuse to lend his services to a patient in dire need of them.

So McConnell thinks that changes in morality occur as a result of changed perspectives supported by reinforcing methods. Therefore, preachment alone is not sufficient to bring about any planned social change. The failure of many radical movements is due to their lack of productive methods by which to deliver the promises of the preachments. In other words, unless the philosophy of a movement is backed up by concrete techniques that bring improved results, the movement is likely to fail.

Skinner is convinced that he has both of the above requirements: a sound description of human behavior which includes a particular perception of the person-environment relationship, plus a set of techniques to reap a greater harvest of rewards.

According to the above considerations, it is incorrect to think that the Skinnerian plan depends upon deception and secret manipulations that will cause people to do things deemed good for them without their knowledge or consent. It is much better to bring the whole plan out into the open, to persuade people that it is a worthy one, and to exhibit its success publicly. If and when these phases come to pass, our future may well be cast in the Skinnerian pattern.

Let us now look at another side of the plan. The moral tone of the Skinnerian movement finds its focus in the belief that control of behavior based on threat and punishment is essentially wrong, and that what is desirable amounts to the development of social behavior that is mutually reinforcing rather than aversive or punishing. This moral tenet has a wide range of practical implications. For example, the heavy diet of violence found in films is bad particularly when those films depict violence as the principal means of reaping rewards, while the victims are described as foolish or inept. Such models of action put on public display are likely to be appealing, especially to immature audiences. Also, the sexual revolution is probably seen by Skinner as involving too much concentration on behavior that has little instrumental value in promoting the general welfare. While sexual behavior is

undeniably rewarding, excessive focus on sexual performance tends to support indulgence as a desirable practice,
and Skinner's theory implies that indulgence is not an effective means for nurturing good human development. The
reason for that judgment was given in an earlier chapter,
but the matter is worth pursuing in greater detail here.

When rewards are provided immediately for little or no
change in behavior, learning will show scant progress. The
parent who indulges the child by rewarding him while he is
behaving in a demanding, selfish, and thoughtless manner
is bound to foster a growth pattern that has negative social
value. And when millions of parents engage in such indulgent practice, the young generation will grow up to produce
a vulnerable society. Its survival strength will be questionable, because those forms of behavior that make a society
strong require a different means of training. More specifically, the indulgent method of nurture fails to produce what
are normally called virtues, namely, strong patterns of behavior that produces reinforcement for other persons. Such
strong responses depend upon intermittent, rather than continuous, schedules of reinforcement; they tend to occur over
long periods of time even without extrinsic reward. In non-
Skinnerian terms, we can say that a virtue is a stable or
enduring trait that is manifested as a means of rewarding
others without expectancy of any immediate payment in
kind. For example, the caring mother who tends to the needs
of her child has the trait of dependability, a strong tendency
to serve the child even under very difficult conditions. The
trouble with indulgence and with continuous schedules of
reinforcement is that they fail to produce much response
strength, and they fail to shape dependable habits that are
reinforcing to others.

It is often believed that mothering is simply an instinct,
a trait provided by nature that requires little if any training.
But that belief may be open to question when it is examined

in certain settings. For example, the Ik society, a tribe of Africans in upper Uganda, show scant regard for their children, turning them out to fend for themselves at about three years of age. In fact, the Ik have lost virtually all habit patterns that can be deemed altruistic. Members of the tribe who become sick and who cannot care for themselves are left to starve. No care is given to the old who can no longer forage on their own. Such traits as love, charity, and compassion have little if any value in Ik society. Even when their fields produce good crops the Ik store no food, despite the fact that most deaths are due to starvation. Much of their food is supplied by the Uganda government in the form of relief packages. The Ik are required to walk a considerable distance to obtain these packages. Those who are strong enough to make the trip consume the food themselves without sharing it with members of their own family who often die of starvation. It is questionable that the Ik can survive much longer in a system that is based on self-indulgence and bereft of altruistic forms of behavior. Their plight is a quite recent phenomenon, because about thirty-five years ago they had a rather robust society, a cohesive organization of nomadic hunters. But suddenly they were forced to settle in a particular region and they had to depend upon farming as their principal means of livelihood. Somehow that sudden change served to extinguish altruistic behavior in the tribe, and their habits quickly degenerated into a pattern of self-indulgence of an extreme sort. The result is a society that reflects less mutual care than is found among families of lower animals. An extended account of the Ik was reported by Turnbull in his book *The Mountain People* (Simon and Schuster, 1972).

Skinner's psychology implies that no social system can survive very long if there is little or no concern for others and if the system provides no reward for being future-oriented, for practicing self-control, and for being productive. What is called "self-actualization" cannot be produced through self-indulgence or by any fad or technique that fails to shape mutually reinforcing behaviors and to strengthen them by intermittent schedules.

The most prominent weakness of the indulgent mode of upbringing is that parents fail to use discrimination in providing reinforcement. Indulgent parents reward children when the latter are being impulsive, demanding, surly, indolent, and the like. Such use of reinforcement fails to produce good progress in what we often call "personality growth." Hence, the trouble with indulgence is that it tends to reinforce immature behavior by not making rewards contingent upon improvement toward more mature patterns. Also, the permissive practice fails to employ the great power of intermittent schedules of reinforcement in a proper fashion. You will recall that the intermittent schedules amount to a variety of ways to dispense rewards so as to establish increased strength of response patterns. Rewards are given intermittently on the basis of either the amount of work performed or the time elapsed, according to a given schedule. Many combinations of intermittent schedules have been established by Skinner and his co-workers. Each schedule can be demonstrated to produce a particular record of performance. In general, the psychological effect is the formation of frustration tolerance, or the ability to persevere even when the reward pattern is thin. Response strength is measured by how long a person will continue working without extrinsic reward.

Traits such as honesty, dependability, courage, love, and the like cannot become fully serviceable unless they are developed in strength. That is, they become most useful only when firmly established as habitual. Therefore, they require a history of intermittent reinforcement plus broad support in the social community. If children grow up to think that impulsiveness, violence, self-centeredness, and dishonesty are more productive of rewards than what we call the virtues, they will fail to acquire the latter. And such learning will dilute the cohesive elements that give society its integrity.

The basic moral value in the Skinnerian system is survival. And survival depends upon the kinds of habit patterns that prevail within the society. Essentially, those patterns must yield mutual reinforcement with a tolerable or minimum amount of aversive consequences.

We are now in a position to estimate some of the major features of the Skinnerian Society. Perhaps the best way of getting a good appraisal of the operant society is to begin with the claims of its supporters and then look at those claims critically. Of course, the entire venture will amount to only a set of approximations or reasonable guesses based on what is known. We seek a balanced estimate for the obvious reason that we want to suppress distortion through bias. With these considerations in mind, let us try to map the territory and to avoid the pitfalls that await both the disciples of the movement and those opponents who are prejudiced in the opposite direction.

THE OPERANT SOCIETY AS VIEWED
BY THE PRO-SKINNERIANS

We must first recognize clearly why the operant plan as applied to the larger society cannot be anything like the *Walden II* model described by Skinner. *Walden II* was a fictitious, small, and almost self-contained community. It was located in a rural setting surrounded by a mass of traditional communities. Because of its small size and carefully selected population, its chief engineer and architect, Frazier, could exercise control in a way that seemed theoretically possible. But when the operant plan is applied to our huge, sprawling, and complex agglomeration of urban and rural communities, the approach must be quite different from the *Walden II* model. The power structure of our nation is composed of many factors that tend to strike a balance or compromise so as to give movement and direction to an evolving life style within a technological setting. Fortunately, we are not under the domination of a single person, such as a Hitler, Stalin, Mao, or Castro. Consequently, the problem facing the operant plan is how to build acceptance of it among the many contrasting factions that compose our society. As noted before, the gradual, piecemeal approach seems to be the most plausible alternative under existing conditions. It must be open and aboveboard, and it must concentrate on the use of certain methods to deal with specific problems. And during the application phase, it must yield results that are distinctly more reinforcing than those provided by past and present efforts. Hence it should be quite obvious that the operant plan cannot be equated with the *Walden II* plan.

Let us begin with a look at some of the economic features of the Skinnerian society. These features will be drawn from Skinner's treatment of "economic control."

Economics has a psychological foundation, namely, those systems of behavior that produce, distribute, and consume goods and services. "Goods" connotes things that are good or useful, such as food, clothing, shelter, luxuries, and the like. Psychologically, they are reinforcers. Also, the word "wealth" suggests a healthy or well state characterized by prosperity, or an abundance of reinforcers. An undesirable economic system is one whose productive efforts are insufficient to meet the "needs" of the people, one in which deprivation prevails. Deprivation is simply a set of conditions characterized by an inadequate level of consumption (insufficient use of necessary reinforcers).

Economics, as a discipline, does not deal with the individual and his specific behavior, nor with the associated contingencies of reinforcement and punishment that produce its basic phenomena. Instead, economists work at a more general level; they speak of buying, selling, lending, borrowing, renting, leasing, hiring, and working, involving millions of people. Skinner writes: "The data include the quantities and location of goods, labor, money, the numbers of economic transactions in a given period, certain characteristics of transactions expressed as costs, prices, interest rates, and wages, together with changes in any of these as functions of time and other conditions." Yet all such data arise from individual patterns of behavior, and their meaning lies in the valuing process that is rooted in reinforcement and punishment. Money, for example, is a generalized conditioned reinforcer, meaning that its value is learned by associations with primary reinforcers, including food, clothing, shelter, and the like, and that it can be used in exchange for a great variety of both primary and secondary reinforcers.

Human labor in the modern world is complex because so many conditions influence it. It functions as a part of a trade-off system, in the sense that one is willing to exchange so much of his labor for a certain income. But other important factors enter the picture: relationships with co-workers, the kind of boss supervising the job, health conditions in the work environment, fringe benefits, the amount of reinforcement found in the work itself, the distance that one must commute, and so on. The boss may use various kinds and degrees of threat to control the workers, his main weapon being the threat of dismissal. Other aversive conditions are usually present. So the worker tries to strike a balance between the assets and discomforts of his job. He is prone to do only that amount of work that will allow him to avoid dismissal; that is, he tends to operate on the principal of minimum output, a level just at the point that will keep the boss "off his neck." However, when the job itself is rewarding the amount of threat needed for control is minimal, because the worker keeps busy without external goads. The craftsman, for example, is influenced not only by the pay he receives but also by his ability to control the medium of his production. When considerable reinforcement is produced in the process of performing a job, the job contains intrinsic reward. Many people in the professions work long hours because they get reinforcement in doing particular tasks central to their occupation. But a person on an assembly line, moving at a fixed rate, is likely to be under aversive control, because the repetitiveness of his simple task tends to yield little satisfaction and because his rate of work is coerced by external means. So his quality of production tends to be just above the level that would cause dismissal.

Economic control is generally aversive. Such control is unpleasant for the worker to the degree that he is "tied to the job" while preferring other activities. But the worker stays on the job if he can strike a balance between aversive and reinforcing conditions. Even the employer is plagued with aversive stimulation, which he also tends to balance against the reinforcement of profit. A simple business deal involves balancing the amount of money that the purchaser is willing to give up against the value of the article or service purchased. Thus, money becomes a common dimension for valuing all sorts of things. The extent that one values something depends upon a variety of factors, particularly upon his deprivation. A very hungry man, for example, is usually willing to spend more for a meal than one who is much less hungry. In general, the supply and distribution of money will somewhat determine the prices of goods and services.

Buying behavior is strengthened when the consequences that are rewarding clearly exceed the aversiveness in paying the price. Hence, it seems likely that members of a family who spend money provided by the breadwinner may be particularly reinforced by buying because they are not directly involved in the labor that produces the money. But certain training in budgeting and in discriminative buying can be sufficiently rewarding to induce prudent management of money. "Learning the value of a dollar is the effect of the aversive consequences of parting with a dollar."

While the above outline points up that economic behavior is a part of the science of behavior because it involves contingencies of reinforcement and punishment, the description is far from complete. Yet we know enough of the operant analysis to suggest the kinds of objectives that the Skinner plan implies within the economic sphere of the operant society. Let us take a look at these implications.

First, there would be an effort to reduce the aversive conditions commonly associated with productive labor. For example, assembly lines would be either eliminated or automated because when the human is used on them his output is minimal due to the high amount of repetitiveness, the lack of variety, and the coerced rate of work.

Second, whatever necessary work is found to be most aversive would receive the highest rate of pay, so as to offset the negative effects. This would create a major shift in the structure and functional details of a given business enterprise. It would lead, for example, to the elimination of as much aversive work as possible, and it would tend to alter job designs so that the pattern and conditions of work would yield considerable intrinsic reward with the least aversive effects. Menial tasks, however, that could not be automated or redesigned satisfactorily would be handsomely rewarded, for the reason given above. This would probably create a significant shift in the distribution of wealth, because people doing aversive but necessary work would receive top wages. Whether or not such a change is feasible is not a point for discussion at the moment. The focus here is on the production of jobs and conditions that would generate considerable reward in the process of doing work while maintaining production at an adequate level. Maximum production would *not* be the main goal; rather, the goal would be optimal job satisfaction correlated with *adequate* production. This would amount to a big psychological engineering operation, involving a much more humanistic goal than most humanists are apparently able to perceive in the Skinnerian plan.

Third, those jobs that give the most satisfaction to the worker would yield modest to low pay, because much of the total reinforcement would be found in job performance. For example, people who very much like to teach, to practice medicine, to do research, or to work as craftsmen would be given adequate but relatively low pay. This practice would weed out people who have no love for the work, leaving only the more dedicated persons in certain fields of endeavor.

Fourth, the practices found in merchandising would be changed considerably. Instead of great time and effort being put into advertising and packaging articles so as to inflate desire for products of questionable merit, the art of persuasion, as now used in merchandising, would be applied to more substantial ends. For example, it might be used to advertise the value of learning new skills instead of to stimulate the desire for things. Current advertising tends to create an unnecessarily high level of consumption, and hence overloads the reinforcement system with things that quickly lead to satiation rather than to long-term satisfaction. Perhaps the most enduring source of reinforcement lies in the exercise of judgment and skills that promote long-range consequences of a positive sort. That kind of satisfaction requires the ability to delay immediate gratification, to be future oriented, to develop a set of interlocking objectives that lead to a distant reward. But at the same time the process yields reinforcement when each of the smaller objectives is achieved. Too many here-and-now reinforcers are likely to produce satiation and boredom, particularly when more distant objectives, which give direction and sustain effort over the long haul, are absent.

So to have a meaningful life one needs a relatively distant goal that he values plus a means of achieving progress toward it. That is why religion is such a strong influence on many people. Religion promises an ultimate reward while providing a plan of action and a set of rules for moving toward that goal. The key to what is called "self-actualization" lies in a series of interlocking goals that are pursued effectively so as to yield an accumulative record of achievement. The life of Skinner reflects that pattern. It is clear that he is pursuing a distant objective, namely, to convince others both by argument and by concrete results to give his system a good try in producing freedom from (avoidance of) the threats that loom large and, in general, creating a more reinforcing social organization. His cumulative record so far looks impressive, and it merits close inspection before proper criticism of it can be made.

We have gotten a glimpse of only some of the economic changes that the operant plan implies; a detailed treatment of the matter would probably fill a good-sized volume. But I think that we have captured the flavor and color of the plan enough to show, in a broad way, how the management of economic reinforcers would be conducted in the operant society.

Another large and important aspect of operant management concerns child training. Child development is a matter of building a set of behavior patterns that change appropriately as the child becomes older. The process is largely controlled by parents, siblings, neighbors, teachers, peers, and others, that is, by the social environment that bears directly upon the growing child. The kind of personality that one develops grows out of the behavior repertory that the environment reinforces. In fact, every person has many personalities, because he develops different patterns of action for different conditions. The way a child behaves at home may be quite different from the way he interacts with his pals. A person behaves differently in solemn and formal situations than in free-wheeling and informal contexts. A friendly bull session brings out different behavior than a funeral or a church ritual.

While certain habits occur despite radical changes in the environment, many other responses do not remain the same. Hence, a person is actually different under contrasting conditions. Psychologically, a person amounts to what he does. He may have good intentions, but the impact that he has upon others—that is, the effect of his personality—depends upon his actions. Thus, a personality amounts to a complex pattern of behavior. So the task of proper child training is to encourage appropriate forms of behavior for a wide variety of conditions. This can be done only by artful management of reinforcers and by building environments that exhibit certain consistencies in the administration of rules. These consistencies should reflect a coherent set of values, so that the behavior learned in one situation is not fundamentally at odds with other behavior learned in different situations. More specifically, these values refer to how people react to one another, and reflect such traits as politeness, honesty, kindness, and the like. In other words, the kind of social environment needed to bring about good child development is one in which people practice ways of treating one another that maximize mutual reinforcement and minimize aversive forms of action. It is possible to engineer that kind of society by proper use of existing techniques of control. A more specific management of child training consistent with these larger considerations is outlined below.

The very young infant would be given maximum freedom to move about within the limits of his ability, without the encumbrance of excessive clothing or other constraints not essential to his safety. He would be promptly fed in response to his hunger signals. This is a most important practice, which may seem rather trivial but actually has far-reaching consequences. Let us look at the matter more closely. No rigid time schedule would be used for feeding during the early months, for fear of weakening what is ordinarily called "initiative." An inflexible time schedule at that early period could weaken the contingency principle; that is, it could have negative effects like the formation of a "fateful expectancy," the tendency to be too passive, to rely upon providence, luck, or happenstance. The fateful expectancy could also be established by providing rewards in a random fashion, that is, without any correlation with how the child behaves. Skinner does not use the same terms as I have used here, but the meaning is about the same. He wants to nurture and strengthen the innate disposition to emit behavior that produces useful consequences. Therefore, the child needs responsible care—meaning parents that behave in a consistent and reliable fashion—so that the contingency principle is sustained. In other words, consistency in child care strengthens the tendency on the part of the child to emit behavior that produces effective consequences. Inconsistent treatment, on the other hand, will promote the attitude in the child that he can do little or nothing to determine the production of reinforcement. He will then become too passive. So the trouble with inconsistency in child care is that it weakens the foundation of self-control. Consequently, it is inaccurate to think that operant training predisposes the person to become a helpless pawn of the environment. The purpose is quite the contrary, because the ultimate aim of good nurture is to help the child achieve maximum self-control, that is, to help him become aware of those conditions that influence his behavior and at the same time learn how to manipulate those conditions for optimal benefit to himself and to others.

As the child grows, a gradual introduction of delay in reinforcement would be used to strengthen desirable responses. Remnants of immature behavior, relevant to a given age, would be extinguished by being nonreinforced. The claim is that the child can easily learn that immature patterns no longer produce desired results whereas appropriately mature behavior pays off. Such learning depends upon proper and consistent management of rewards.

In the operant society, the child would not be indulged, because of reasons given earlier. Also, permissiveness, when used to mean laissez-faire management by parents, would not occur, as it would be regarded as a parental cop-out. In other words, permissiveness amounts to the rejection of parental control, leaving control to caprice and to the peer group, which may condition some real problem behavior. Permissiveness should not be confused with indulgence, although the two have some common elements. The former, when practiced in extreme form, means that nearly any act is allowed without particular corrective feedback. But the biggest drawback to permissiveness is that no special reinforcement is given for desirable forms of behavior. The parent becomes a somewhat neutral personality. He fails to show consistent positive regard for good behavior and is equally passive about bad behavior. Hence, the parent relinquishes his role as an active agent in the upbringing of the child. In later life, the child may come to resent parental permissiveness and charge the parent with not having had enough concern, that is, with neglect of parental duty. Some children, if not all, seem to need a certain amount of structure imposed by older and more experienced people. Children do not resent rules that give them good guidelines for coping, even though these guidelines may require some rigorous training, as is associated with teaching delay of immediate gratification and frustration tolerance.

In general, the socialization of young people, that is, the shaping of their behavior so that they can function effectively and constructively in social settings, is a kind of brainwashing process. But it is a brainwashing that is necessary for a surviving society, which needs the cohesion supplied by mutual reinforcement. There is no possible way that a person can be socialized without also being controlled by the people in his environment. The person is always easier to change than the whole social system. Hence, it is most convenient and practical to shape the child's behavior so that it is reasonably compatible with that of his associates. Parents should not feel guilty in taking positive steps to control the behavior of their children, because even if they choose the permissive cop-out other persons and groups will inevitably impose control, and probably with much less concern for the child than is found in the average parent.

Another aspect of child training implied by the operant system is an early establishment of work habits. Children can and should learn to do chores at an early age, and they should be trained to help with household work plus other jobs within their abilities. This does not mean that children should be burdened with excessive tasks, but it does mean that they should be encouraged to assume a reasonable amount of work that contributes to the welfare of the whole family. If we want to promote behavior that is mutually reinforcing, the operant argument says, we must begin with the child and teach him to value service to others by having him contribute some of his labor. For example, children can be taught rather early to make their own beds, to keep their toys in order, and to help their parents in other ways. Also, they should take on added responsibilities as they grow older. The psychological importance of such training is perhaps most clearly expressed by reference to the typical rural family of a generation or more ago. In that family children were taught to do work that was valued by all members of the household. The children made real contributions to the economic welfare of the family. They did not need frequent reminders of their worth, someone to "pat them on the back" to bolster their egos. They knew full well their importance, that the family needed their help. No artificial contrivances were necessary to strengthen their self-concepts.

The psychological robustness of the old rural family was

rooted in the fact that it had an integrated reinforcement system. That is, the economic, social, educational, and religious reinforcers formed a rather close-knit structure. Today, however, many reinforcement clusters exist that do not hang together. In order to dip into one reinforcement pool the person may be required to do things that are punished in another setting. For example, a teenager who samples drugs may be supported for doing so by his peers, but the same behavior may be punished in the home and in other contexts. The ease of moving from one source of satisfaction to another is one major feature of the modern age. But the psychological catch to this is that the person needs a means of keeping some of his activities secret from certain groups. The result is that the person lives in several small worlds that are not compatible. He therefore supports the tendency to hold these worlds apart, thus contributing to a kind of social disintegration. If, however, he elects to confine himself to only one oasis of reinforcement, a small subculture, he finds himself increasingly alienated from other parts of the culture. Hence, overall success requires considerable flexibility. But the price paid is internal conflict and erosion of moral values. These considerations make up some of the reasons why the Skinnerians believe that we desperately need a better way of dealing with our psychological problems. Their insight is more penetrating than they are often given credit for. We must try to grasp their message before responding to it critically.

Today's teenagers are occasionally targets of bitter criticism by some journalists and by people with certain attitudes and beliefs. Let us look at a typical set of criticisms of our adolescents to see how the operant psychologist reacts and, particularly, to learn what kind of prescription he has to offer. I shall try to paint a strong indictment against the teenager as subscribed to by his most severe critics. I don't subscribe to it. But the picture runs as follows.

It would be hard to devise a plan of child training that could produce a worse crop of youths than we have now. Just look at their
attitudes, values, and habits! When some people praise them as
our best generation of kids, they must be either blind or crazy.
The stubborn facts suggest that the future of our society will be
a complete disaster unless some miracle happens quite soon. Let's
take a typical family with two or three teenagers living under
ordinary middle-class conditions. In the first place, Mom does all
the housework. She breaks her back keeping things straight while
the lazy kids loll around in their messy rooms listening to a
garbage of sounds they call "music" and gobble up goodies
served by Mom, who cleans up the mess after the kids decide to
take the family car to collect some friends and "tool around,"
overriding the weak request by Mom about wanting the car to
go shopping. The kids are demanding, ill-tempered, thoughtless,
conceited, and disrespectful, and they slide by in their high-
school courses with a minimum of work. They can't stand criticism but are always dishing it out, especially about the big mess
that the older generation has made of the world. They are virtually incapable of original thinking, although they believe that
they are the only truly enlightened and creative people in the
whole society. They mouth platitudes about love and brotherhood without having the remotest notion of what they're talking
about because they have never practiced the sacrifices that make
up the real meaning of both concepts. They have a "liberal"
attitude toward drugs, believing that the use of narcotics is
simply a personal matter. They don't stop to recognize the heart-
ache and embarrassment that drug abuse can cost others. They
preach a "party line" about social justice while engaging in the
most extreme forms of self-indulgence. Their slogan is "freedom,
total freedom." They have no idea of what freedom really is; they
equate it with the maximum amount of immediate pleasure, and
they regard responsibility with some passing degree of verbal
respect without ever having practiced it at all. For kicks they "rip
off" articles that they don't need from local department stores
and regard their feat as striking a blow against the evils of the
"system," without realizing that the ones they hurt most are the
poor, who must pay higher prices to cover the loss. Lying to their

parents is considered an art, and they exchange stories about "psyching out" parents and teachers. The wildest and most successful lie gets the most applause. But in their little fun culture they frequently have feelings that they label "alienation," "loss of identity," "futility," "boredom," "negative self-concept," "powerlessness," and "worthlessness." To cope with such feelings they are alert to all the psychological gimmicks and fads, including a watered down Zen Buddhism or some other equally misconceived occult discipline. They seek the instant satisfaction inculcated by the TV cartoons that were staples of their early training. They are too ignorant to see that the strong, healthy personality that they dream about cannot grow in the field of habits that engulfs them. They are psychologically the weakest generation ever produced in America, and if their children show the same degree of "progress" they might as well turn themselves over to the Chinese or Russians voluntarily, because they will lack the fiber to make it on their own. They harbor the dreamy illusion that the world will somehow sense their great humanistic traits and fall at their feet for guidance and wisdom. Thus, they oscillate wildly between the most unreal expectancies and deep despondency. The fact is that they are really psychotic, but few people have the guts to admit the truth. Reluctance to admit the widespread psychosis among the youth has led to the acceptance of the bizarre notion that crazy people aren't really crazy, the kind of crap voiced by R. D. Laing and others. Of course, when diseased minds threaten to become more numerous than healthy ones, we feel inclined to invent false explanations that will make everybody feel better. But the tragedy of the process is that such inventions don't change the hard facts.

These disturbed adolescents don't have the foggiest notion of the hard realities of life in the Orient and in other parts of the Communist sphere, which they often regard with esteem. They were easily duped by the Jane Fonda stories of how well the North Vietnamese treated American prisoners of war, and they seemed strangely unmoved by later reports of torture from returning prisoners. They don't have the remotest grasp of the prevailing Oriental style of life, which is duty-bound and has little regard for personal rights, creature comforts, and the cream-puff interpretation of humanism. And they don't realize that the spartan life among Communists in Oriental nations predisposes those people to look upon the typical American teenager with disgust and as the epitome of what they seek to avoid in their own society.

One of the most compelling facts that points up the deep phoniness of the typical teenager is that he excels the older generation in practicing the very vices that he verbally deplores. He goes the older generation one better in the way of hypocrisy and self-deceit. For example, there is the sad but true story of the great "love" that college kids have for dogs, and their strong disapproval of anyone who mistreats a dumb animal. They indulge their dogs and give them much attention. But when spring vacation arrives they split for new areas of entertainment, leaving the dogs locked in their apartments to die of thirst and hunger. Scores of dogs in one midwestern college town suffered that "humanistic" fate only recently. And the following fall, the same kids may be easily persuaded to march on the state capitol to demonstrate against the use of animals for medical research! Such blatant inconsistency can hardly be seen as anything but a sign of a serious mental disease. If we continue to close our eyes to these facts, we shall be swept along with the rationalizations used to whitewash such unforgivable behavior.

So when we get to the bare bones of the matter, no one really likes the American teenager, not even the teenager himself. It is hard to see how any deliberate plan could produce a more miserable and worthless crop of kids. We have hit the jackpot—of lemons.

The above account was paraphrased and pieced together from a variety of sources, mostly from newspaper articles. It was constructed, as mentioned before, in order to consider how the operant psychologist would react to it. So let us now turn to his response.

Although the above report supports the operant claim that

we urgently need radical changes in child training, the operant psychologist, because of his loyalty to science and its methods, would be quick to point out weaknesses in it that do not accord with his logic. In the first place, the report deals with teenagers as if they were all the same. So it contains a glaring exaggeration (overgeneralization), simply because there are great differences among adolescents. Certainly all teenagers in America do not conform to the given description, not even all middle-class teenagers. Second, the claim that most if not all teenagers are psychotic is another overstatement. The facts cannot allow putting the label "psychotic" on such a large segment of our society. Third, the account makes only scant reference to actual response patterns, which are telescoped into trait names such as "demanding," "ill-tempered," "conceited," "disrespectful," and the like. The operant psychologist rejects these terms, and similar ones, as too general and lacking in specificity. (Although I have used such terms throughout this book in order to expedite communication, the operant psychologist shuns them.) Fourth, the practice of placing blame on the teenager for his predicament would be avoided, because blaming people for their misdeeds is a futile activity. It is much better to examine the actual behavior and decide what parts of it ought to be changed, and then to go about the task systematically, with operant tools.

Given these initial reservations, the operant man would place some credence in the report, because it does refer to behaviors that call for modification. For example, teenagers were seen as failing to help in the housework when such help was clearly needed, giving aversive reactions to their parents, seeking all the immediate reinforcers that they could consume, wavering in thoughts about themselves from great admiration to despair, having distorted notions about Orientals, and treating dogs in a thoughtless and deadly way. The first task is to translate these events into contingencies of reinforcement, so that a proper analysis of them can be made. The report fails to give us sufficient data on the matter, but it would be possible to examine actual cases and determine a clear-cut analysis. Since we do not have the necessary facts, suffice it to say that the operant psychologist would approach the larger problem by the preventive route; that is, he would advise starting early with the right form of child training. Also, he would probably suspect that the undesirable behavior traits mentioned in the report stem from an indulgent or permissive mode of upbringing. But even an adolescent, brought up under poor training methods, could be helped, provided parents would learn operant techniques and use them consistently. Also, the teenagers themselves should be taught operant psychology, and they should be managed so that reinforcement would be contingent upon their learning it. When all members of the family are properly educated, they can aid one another in shaping the kind of conduct that they deem most desirable.

In summary, the child training implied by the Skinner plan involves the use of operant methods to condition children to acquire those moral behaviors that are consistent with the moral tone of the movement as outlined near the beginning of this chapter. These morals include a good portion of the old-fashioned virtues, because the latter are deemed useful for social cohesion, which depends upon mutually reinforcing social habits. The big departure from traditional training lies in the scientific means of establishing and maintaining the target behaviors.

A third important side of the operant plan besides economic behavior and child rearing, concerns education. Operant education has a clear-cut structure, including a list of goals couched in action words, programmed texts, the use of tokens for rewarding proper responses while "bad" conduct goes unreinforced, and a systematic use of the new media. Learning tasks are selected so that they are well within the child's ability to perform. They stimulate frequent activity on the part of the learner, who is given corrective information immediately so that he can judge and change his performance. Thus learning and self-testing are combined, so that an account can be given of the student's progress at any given time. The student does not attempt a new task until he has mastered the preceding one, while getting all the help he needs. Each child progresses at his own pace.

Education is seen as a human engineering process, and teachers become technologists who understand the principles of operant learning and who manage the environment so that failure approaches zero. It is a form of individualized education that contrasts sharply at many points with open education or the "open classroom" approach, which has been growing rapidly in the past few years. The open educators accept a set of values that reflect the new version of humanism. For example, many of them believe that human nature is basically good; therefore, if children are given many options along with a rather lax system of supervision, they will eventually develop good social habits, learn an adequate amount of knowledge and skills, and, above all, acquire responsibility and self-direction. They will also become more creative than students in the more structured schools.

Operant psychologists look at these claims of open education with considerable skepticism. Their reasons are multiple. First, human nature cannot be shown to be basically either good or bad. There is no compelling evidence that confirms one theory of human nature and discomfirms the others. It is much more practical to deal with concrete problems of behavior than to wallow amidst the uncertainties of theories on human nature. Second, it is unlikely that very young children are capable of making important decisions about what they should learn or not learn, because they have insufficient knowledge to accurately project their own needs even a short time into the future. Development of the skill needed to make such complex judgments can come only gradually, through cumulative learning. It is a good target to shoot for, but it cannot be assumed as acquired at an early age. The interests of youngsters are whimsical, and any system that caters to their interests to the point of indulgence will simply reinforce impulsiveness. In summary, most open-classroom procedures reflect a profound ignorance of the learning process and how it should be managed. The good parts of it can be easily incorporated into the operant approach, and by so doing many disappointing outcomes can be avoided.

The plan promises that whatever skills, knowledge, and values the community wants to instill in young people, within the school setting, can be accomplished more effectively by operant techniques than by any past or present methods of another sort. The big aim of operant education is to design a clear-cut curriculum that is consistent with the operant morality. Teaching should become a technology, or the art of applying the science of human behavior. It should service society and should not attempt to become a spearhead for initiating and carrying out social change, because ultimate control of the schools does not rest in the hands of teachers, administrators, and students, but in the larger community. The ultimate goal of education is to help the child become an effective learner by equipping him with useful knowledge and skills and by helping him achieve the kind of self-control that is compatible with those values and practices needed in order for a society to survive and prosper.

Although there are several other aspects of the operant plan that have not been covered, only one more will be treated here, namely, government. By adding some estimates regarding the operant government, we should have a sufficiently good picture of Skinner's overall objectives.

From the operant point of view, government is composed of a hierarchy of officials who make decisions about what is

legal or illegal, who judge events in terms of the laws en-
acted, and who execute plans to maintain the system.
Government is involved mainly with power, which can be
managed badly or wisely. The soundest management of
power accords with the principles of the science of human
behavior (operant psychology), and contains practices that
promote strong mutual reinforcement in everyday affairs.
But the ideal government is one which succeeds in making
its use of power increasingly unnecessary. When the home
has a sound set of nurturing practices, when education operates successfully, when moral behavior forms a strong, mutually reinforcing system, and when economic arrangements
minimize the aversiveness in productive work, a strong central government that wields power in a threatening manner
is needed only in cases of emergency. This viewpoint is
reminiscent of Confucius and his doctrine of government.
Skinner claims that we are now in striking distance of that
ideal because we have the knowledge and techniques that
can be used to make it a reality. Let us look at some of the
specific changes that would be attempted under the operant
plan.

One of the first moves of the operant government would
be to publicize and encourage the adoption of improved
child-training practices, as outlined above. It would probably be necessary to make use of power during the early
stages in order to stimulate action. The main strategy would
involve rewarding parents who show evidence of using the
proper training procedures. A wide variety of possibilities
could be used to carry out that strategy. For example, it
might be effective to extend to successful parents sizeable
tax exemptions on the grounds that good child training
would reduce the amount of revenue necessary to maintain
our huge penal and correctional institutions, which would
dwindle in size as the plan succeeds over the years. Also, it
is possible that parents who fail in the training program

would bear the brunt of supporting the penal institutions; but they would be given help and encouragement in child training by local agencies geared for such service. In general, a new set of tax loopholes would emerge to benefit those citizens who contribute effectively to the child-training program. Such favors would extend to all persons, whether parents or not, who strengthen and abet the program. Thus, special incentives would arise to attract persons to educate themselves in this field.

Second, a careful examination of existing laws would be made to identify those that do not function as intended. Many laws seem to be dysfunctional in the sense that they are commonly broken and create considerable expense in the failing effort to enforce them. The Volstead Act, which prohibited the sale of hard liquor, is a good case in point. Perhaps more than any other single event, that law stimulated the growth of the underworld syndicates that are now said to control huge enterprises of both a legal and an illegal nature. The most effective means of combatting organized crime is simply to arrange conditions so that the activities of the syndicates no longer pay off. This process may involve the repealing of certain laws that are easy and profitable to break. For example, one bold move might involve the removal of drug abuse laws, which prove so profitable to those who traffic in narcotics. But the legalization of drugs would have to be combined with a vigorous training program that minimized the reinforcement obtained by those who elected to use drugs. Alternatives to drugs could be developed that would provide equally gratifying effects without harmful results. One such possibility *might* lie in the rising use of biofeedback, which amounts to a set of techniques for translating and amplifying internal bodily processes so that the person can monitor them through audible sounds or visual stimuli. Although no one seems to know just why biofeedback works, there is limited evidence that some people can learn to control certain physiological functions so as to escape headaches and other pains, including stomach ulcers and similar psychic diseases. Also, biofeedback seems to offer a person the promise of a wide range of self-control, which could lead to a variety of pleasant states, rivaling and even surpassing the reinforcement provided by hard drugs.

A third move of the operant government would be an attempt to change the threat system that has existed for so long in international politics. Instead of engaging in wars of the Vietnam type, we would concentrate on exporting information about our success in getting rid of dependence of threat and punishment as means of control. Many people in foreign lands already prefer our system despite its defects, suggesting that other societies are less reinforcing and more punitive than our own. The operant plan would probably bank on the notion that if we can demonstrate great success in mastering our own problems, our way of life would need no military display of power in order to persuade people to accept it. In fact, so the operant argument goes, the more we depend upon wielding the big stick, the less likely we will be to succeed in our quest to convince others to adopt our way of life. Remember, effective innovation must deliver a new perspective and improved returns in reinforcement. Once those two aspects are effectively displayed, imitation will follow. Innovation will be accepted without strife.

But the operant plan would maintain an investment in the national defense until it became clear that no other power could use force in preventing the successful completion of the plan. The expectation, however, would be that the need for huge armaments would rapidly decline as the success of the plan became apparent.

Government would be involved in the economic sphere by exerting its influence to discourage unnecessary production, particularly the production of goods and services that threaten successful implementation of the plan. For example, high-powered, fast cars would probably vanish from the market because they stimulate behavior that leads to injury and death. Everyone deplores the great slaughter on our highways, but little is done to control the behavior that produces the high rate of accidents. The most effective control of that source of danger would be to make it impossible to own a car capable of high speeds and to make issuance of a driver's license contingent upon safe performance. Again, the reinforcement system could assert its power by rewarding safe drivers with a significant reduction in the price of a car and of gasoline and other expenses associated with driving. It would be possible to make the reward differential between safe and unsafe drivers so great that careless driving would become virtually extinct. The trouble with the existing control system is that careless drivers have little incentive to change their ways, because the reinforcement for driving in a daring fashion is not overpowered by incentives to drive carefully. Unless the reinforcement contingencies are changed radically, we will continue to have a small percentage of drivers responsible for the majority of accidents.

The effort to reduce unnecessary production would have a double advantage: it would both result in reduced pollution and help promote a shift in values. Excessive production of goods that promise here-and-now gratification while reducing the chance of building frustration tolerance and a future orientation would be seen as noise in the system, to be sharply reduced. In other words, it would be bad psychology to manage a society so as to encourage operant morality while increasing incentives that would cancel the desired effects. So it would be necessary to control the number and kinds of alternatives available in everyday affairs. Self-indulgent options, for example, would be hard to maintain. The operant plan would minimize those alternatives that lead to aversive or harmful consequences. Hence, the kind of freedom that would be curtailed would be freedom to harm or injure one's self or others. But the curtailment would not exist as a threat system; rather, it would be inherent in the strong conditioning of desirable behavior. There would be little if any social support for responses antithetical to the approved mores.

The influence of government would be needed to stimulate action toward altering the pay rates for different kinds of work. The necessary drudgery performed by garbage collectors, assembly-line laborers, nurses' aides, and other workers who perform important but unpleasant tasks would be pushed near the top of the pay scale. These toilers could retire with a comfortable income after less sustained work than people who do more pleasant tasks. The effort would be to balance the total reinforcement across the various kinds of jobs. Such a change would tend to create a different attitude toward labor. But in the long run technology would be used to eliminate aversive tasks as much as possible, so that more people could engage in jobs that yield a variety of reinforcers. The net result might be a reduction in the power of money.

SUMMARY OF LIFE IN THE OPERANT SOCIETY

The foregoing speculations suggest the kind of world that the Skinnerian plan would attempt to produce within a large modern society. The picture presented is a favorable one, which harmonizes with the spirit and principles of operant psychology. The constraints of current conditions account for the sharp differences between the above account and the *Walden II* description.

Before a critique of the operant society is attempted, I shall summarize the seven main features of the system just covered.

1. The general pace of living would be slower in the operant community than under current conditions. Reduc-

tion of persuasive advertising stimulating overbuying and re-duced production of questionable articles and services would bring a marked decline in the "busyness" of the environment. Use of the mass media to condition people to desire all sorts of superficial things would be sharply curtailed.

2. Dependence upon threat and punishment for control-ling behavior would be minimized.

3. Operant child-training methods would be used to shape altruistic patterns of behavior. Permissiveness and indul-gence would be virtually eliminated as modes of child man-agement.

4. An increase in job satisfaction would be promoted by redesigning jobs so as to reduce monotony and boredom. The net result would be increased reinforcement in the per-formance of productive tasks.

5. The present trend towards fragmentation of the moral code would be reversed by using operant techniques to establish a homogeneous set of social values.

6. Cooperative behavior would be shaped to strengthen awareness of interdependence by promoting a strong mutual-reinforcement pattern in the family, in the school, and in the economic world.

7. The present legal structure would be streamlined and simplified so that less and less dependence would be put on written laws. Common law would eventually predominate in all phases of society.

In general, social change would occur by first using oper-ant analysis to determine desirable behavior modification and then applying the techniques of the psychology to realize each objective. One of the most important changes is that the mature adult would acquire a maximum level of self-control, according to the operant perspective.

A CRITIQUE OF THE OPERANT PLAN

The above account is a reasonably good estimate of what the operant psychologist would expect to happen if his plan were adopted. The big question is: what are the weaknesses of the plan, if any? My answer is basically simple; *the plan places too much dependence on the deterministic assumption.* Although I have tried to explain the value of cognitive freedom and why its omission in the plan is a serious one, I think that a more detailed treatment of the matter is needed.

In the first place, a rigid insistence on determinism along with an equally rigid rejection of self-autonomy can be seen as both unnecessary and inaccurate. Also, people just do not like the idea that their behavior is completely determined. Therefore, so long as the operant plan remains rigidly deterministic, the first phase of the plan—persuading people that it should be given a good try—may be quite difficult, although not impossible. But the main defect is not in promoting an uncomplimentary perspective of human behavior, however difficult it may be to win its acceptance; rather, the weakness lies in clinging to a position that cannot be maintained by the available evidence. Such is the crux of my criticism. Now, let us examine the considerations that support the criticism.

Let us recall Bridgman's "solution" to the freedom-determinism dilemma. Bridgman said that we need both freedom and determinism because part of our world requires a freedom frame of reference while another part requires a deterministic one. The former is necessary when we cannot predict with any degree of assurance. Everyday life is so complicated that we cannot possibly know precisely what we will do next month, next week, or even in the next five minutes. Before the deterministic assumption can be useful, it must work. There is no value in using determinism if we cannot make it a valid basis for action. And there are almost countless situations in which we are so limited. We may *think* that our world operates in a determined fashion, but that thought does little good when we are helpless in putting it to work. In the laboratory, the scientist finds it quite useful to assume determinism because of the great control he has over conditions and because his problems are conceived within the deterministic framework.

The deterministic assumption, however, not only is useful in the laboratory, but is also important in dealing with many everyday tasks. For example, a cake cannot be made with much expectancy of success unless one believes in and behaves according to determinism. A certain proportion of ingredients mixed a certain way and baked in an oven at the proper heat level for a particular length of time—all these determine an edible product. Skinner is on firm ground when he uses his system to deal with problems that require the deterministic assumption. But unfortunately, he overextends his faith in determinism by tackling problems that involve overwhelming errors of prediction, as for example his analysis of creativity, mentioned earlier in the book.

All deterministic psychologies are weak in making accurate predictions about cognitive behavior, particularly in the area of "creative problem solving." Creativity is a thorn in the side of the determinist because he finds that it eludes his efforts to pin it down as a concrete process and because he can do little to predict and control the creative act. Yet he cannot deny the existence of countless instances of originality. Newton's production of the binomial theorem, invention of calculus, and development of the laws of mechanics are best labeled "creative" because they cannot be accepted as routine and cannot be regarded as purely accidental. But just what process Newton used can only be dimly perceived. And the great impact of his accomplishments can hardly be exaggerated. So we are left with a phenomenon that must be accepted as quite significant, as something very real, but also as something that defies adequate explanation within the deterministic context.

We have no way of conditioning creative behavior. So when we stick to the known facts, we must entertain the idea that *creativity is something that exists because determinism is limited.* We know that mental habits can be so strong that they block off recognition of even obvious solutions to problems. The story about the semi-trailer that was lodged tightly between the road and a bridge ceiling is a good case in point. A battery of experts, including an engineer or two, had applied their efforts without success when a small boy suggested that some air should be removed from the tires. Following the boy's suggestion, the driver easily freed the truck and went happily on his way. The creative person must somehow free himself from strong popular beliefs, from common channels of thought, and from certain habitual associations of concepts. Just how he accomplishes that freedom has not been clearly ascertained. There seems to be no deterministic logic that provides us with a promising approach for handling creativity. But if we use the freedom assumption, we can say that the person has some degree of autonomy, that he can choose to challenge established lore, and by so doing can produce something unorthodox, yet meaningful and useful. The freedom conception does no violence to what is known, although it does not satisfy the determinist. But it is possible that any attempt to deal with creativity by deterministic means will remain awkward and unsatisfactory. We can hardly help but feel that we do have some measure of latitude in many situations, that we are not purely limited by the environment. Because we have that feeling and because the deterministic approach has not yet proved adequate in handling all psychological phenomena, it seems a bit extreme to rule out autonomy altogether.

It is important to realize that no claim is being made to deny the usefulness of operant procedures for dealing with deterministic problems. I am only insisting that we keep in mind one obvious fact, namely, that not all psychological problems have been proved agreeable to deterministic methods. Consequently, it is necessary to maintain that the operant plan is not as universally applicable as its supporters seem to assume.

Even some concepts in operant psychology can be considered as requiring both the freedom and deterministic notions. For example, the operant response and self-control are defined by Skinner so as to leave some room for self-autonomy, although they are used by him only within the deterministic framework. One important feature of operant behavior is that no initial stimulus can be identified that gives rise to the operant response, which is said to be emitted rather than *evoked*. Skinner adopts the idea that much behavior is emitted, in that he rejects the efforts of other behaviorists who try to account for the initial expression of each response by trying to find its stimulus antecedent. He claims that such efforts are futile, and so he simply accepts the operant as a given fact, concentrating his attention on what conditions are correlated with changes in the frequency of the operant. Obviously, his scheme leaves the door wide open for introducing freedom or autonomy as a possible explanation of how the operant is initiated. The problem is not solved simply be refusing to deal with it, as Skinner elects to do. He concentrates on subsequent changes in operant strength by developing functional relationships of a deterministic sort. But the very notion of autonomy concerns itself with the origin of behavior, the problem of how ideas and acts first come into existence. The operant system does not address itself to that problem, which is the very point most relevant to the whole issue. So we can say that Skinner has limited himself only to those facts and tasks that can be fitted into his deterministic scheme. Skinner's deliberate limitation implies that his deterministic approach cannot deal with a very important problem without using some doubtful speculations. Consequently, his position does not rule out autonomy with any good degree of assurance. He is quite aware of the fact that he cannot demonstrate, so far, the universal validity of determinism. But that very recognition means that determinism is not yet sufficient for handling all important problems of a psychological sort; that is, both prediction and control break down at certain points. Bridgman wisely suggests that when determinism proves inadequate, it is both convenient and useful to shift to the freedom assumption. So if we take Bridgman's advice, we see that even the operant psychologists can remain on firmer ground if they simply admit when a shift to the freedom assumption is in order. Of course, they are certainly free to think that further research will strengthen their faith in determinism. But they should not confuse faith with facts. The upshot of all this is that the very important concept of operant behavior is not fundamentally confined to a deterministic interpretation. Therefore, it seems logical to adopt a more flexible position than that held by the Skinnerians.

A similar analysis can be made of operant self-control. It is not necessary to go into a detailed examination of the concept here. Suffice it to say that one's decision to exercise control over variables that in turn influence his behavior cannot be fully demonstrated as deterministic.

What impact do these points have on the operant plan? The main effect is that they introduce moderation concerning the results that can be expected. They suggest that we should anticipate some difficulties that are not emphasized by Skinner. It is not likely that the plan can be executed smoothly and without considerable cut-and-try procedures. But it is possible that the plan can eventually produce a fair approximation of its goals if the theory is made more flexible by admitting cognitive freedom and if its methods are modified accordingly. If the theory is changed to give cognitive freedom its due recognition, Phase One of the plan would become much easier because it would relieve people of the fear of being manipulated without their consent. Although that fear is largely fictitious, an emphasis upon cognitive freedom would probably dispel it. Also, recognition of cognitive freedom would help square the theory with certain realities, particularly those limitations of deterministic psychology that concern the breakdown of prediction and control in the field of creative behavior and related cognitive activities. It is both good psychology and good science to admit the limitations of a given proposal. I do not think that Skinner has given sufficient emphasis to the doubtful aspects of his plan. If he would do so he would be more modest in his prescription. He would de-emphasize the utopian implications and give more recognition to the hurdles and uncertainties that stand in the way. But even when these changes are introduced, there is much promise and hope in the plan. In fact, the suggested changes may, in improving the soundness of the plan, make it more realistic.

Although my effort to examine the operant plan contains some "iffy" assumptions and interpretations, I think that it represents essentially the kind of approach that is needed to deal effectively with any serious idea or movement. Those who uncritically accept good-sounding proposals and who rush into action are almost always headed for some bitter disenchantment. On the other hand, those who rigidly reject new ideas without first taking the trouble to study them and grasp them fully are suppressing their educational growth. Good education, I believe, requires taking the middle course between the two extremes. Effective education must include more than exposure to information. It must involve skills in handling information, namely, the arts of analysis, criticism, and putting parts together to form conclusions.

In my effort to use those cognitive skills in appraising Skinner's position, I find that the outcome is not nearly as dreary as that indicated in the purely negative criticisms, nor is it as rosy as the picture painted by the uncritical disciples of the movement. An honest effort to exercise cognitive freedom often yields results that are neither too gloomy nor too optimistic. I like to think that sound education requires considerable use of cognitive freedom.

FOR FURTHER READING

SKINNER, B. F. *Science and Human Behavior*. New York: Macmillan Company, 1953.

Epilogue

In this modern world of increasing change, good mental health depends more and more on cognitive freedom. In the few remaining pages I would like to examine some points that bear upon this claim.

We live in a pluralistic society, meaning that many contrasting systems of beliefs, values, and patterns of behavior co-exist without any single system that is clearly predominant. In other words, we live in a highly differentiated society that offers many modes of living, and the individual is faced with the problem of which mode to select. It is fashionable nowadays to say that each person ought to discover his own life style and live accordingly, regardless of what others may think. Additional items of this currently popular philosophy include the following: (a) Life is a short one-shot affair and should not be wasted on any so-called noble sacrifices. Pleasure is the central value in life and it comes only to those who take it. (b) Each person is unique; he is no carbon copy of anyone else. Therefore, he should seek what is especially good for himself—his own life style. (c) The most fitting life style for a given person can be found only by sampling a wide variety of experiences directly, firsthand. (d) In this search one should not be shackled by traditional values, mores, or even laws that constrain freedom to experience whatever appears attractive. (e) Nothing exists except the present; the past is dead, and the future never comes. Whatever is worthwhile can occur only now. (f) We should not be concerned about what another person does because that is his business and none of our own. Live and let live. (g) Feeling, intuition, and impulse are better sensing devices of pleasure than reflective thought, which only blunts the intensity of joy and ecstasy. If epitaphs on graves were still popular, none would be more highly esteemed than: "[So-and-so] really lived."

The above doctrine puts a premium on personal freedom, which has a particular meaning, *viz.*, the absence of internal and external constraint. Two conditions are necessary for this kind of freedom: existence of a wide variety of ready-made alternatives and the lack or relative lack of internal inhibition. It presupposes a state of affairs that can be dubbed the "easy option." The ideal environment of this sort is a secular Garden of Eden with all its goodies, but bereft of rules and regulations of a higher power or any other central authority. One simply picks and chooses whatever pleases him. It is an eternal picnic or orgy, whichever one prefers. Amusement must not be interrupted by muse-ment, by serious thought.

The easy option style of life would be quite feasible except for one flaw, which has nothing to do with any preachment or theory of ethics. This flaw is an inherent aspect of the world of experience. It lies in the simple fact that we often make mistakes, and the consequences of some mistakes keep dogging us later on; we cannot shed them like a garment. Since we don't live in a secular Garden of Eden, we have to be content with something less perfect. Our choices are often faulty in the sense that they yield outcomes less desirable than expected. But this imperfection could be easily tolerated if it were not for the fact that some errors produce results that cling to our backs like monkeys. Some mistakes are irreversible, which means that they cannot be undone. For example, a person may choose certain friends who lead him into activities that he dislikes. Although the person wants to free himself from the activities, his companions may deny that privilege on the ground that the exodus of any member may endanger the whole group enterprise. Some people have become drug addicts and later tried to break the habit, because it proved less desirable than first anticipated. But despite heroic measures to quit the drug, many cannot escape its control. It becomes a permanent millstone on the neck of the victim.

One basic defect in the easy option philosophy lies in the nature of impulse, which by definition is action without reflection. Impulse would be acceptable if all available alternatives were of a positive sort. But, unfortunately, reality does not limit its sphere of events to only those that produce pleasure.

Another weakness in this most naive form of hedonism is the assumption that pleasure is purely physical in nature. This is obviously false, because it omits, among other things, the intense satisfaction that comes from creative work, from overcoming obstacles to achieve a maximum effect as found in the arts.

Relative to genuine freedom, the most serious flaw in this so-called life style is that it delivers its believers into the hands of determinists, who find it easy to predict and control those who depend on impulse in the pursuit of physical pleasure. The most easily exploited people are those driven only by basic appetites and who, on ideological grounds, reject reason. Whatever freedom they may claim to have is largely illusory, the kind that Skinner labels "fictitious."

The point of all these remarks is that naive hedonism, which is inferior to the more substantial forms of that philosophy, is that it rests on a gross misconception of reality. It therefore provides a faulty basis for action and serves to inhibit the very success that it seeks to achieve. Poor reaction to reality is about the only reliable basis for determining what we call "mental disease." Although the concept "insanity" has been criticized on the ground that its users fail to comprehend the real nature of the phenomena to which they refer, there is no doubt that some patterns of coping are inferior, and that some people exhibit a progressive deterioration in their efforts to cope. When they are helped to find more effective means of behaving, they almost universally show gratitude. All styles of coping are not equally satisfying; some of them produce far more misery than pleasure.

The exercise of cognitive freedom lies in the application of certain skills: ability to make reasonably accurate observations, ability to identify important relationships within patterns of experience, ability to control impulse, ability to make accurate deductions from firm premises, ability to draw sound conclusions from limited facts; also to analyze, synthesize, and evaluate. These skills are within the potential of virtually all people, except those who are hopelessly brain-damaged. But they take some time to develop; and above all they require delay of gratification. Without them the person is usually an easy target for various means of exploitation, such as certain kinds of propaganda, unethical advertising, image-making, promotion schemes, and the like.

Mental health not only means the absence of psychological illness, it also connotes a gusto for life, an eagerness to deal with challenge, an ability to adjust, and skill in managing conditions to promote worthwhile aims. It is clear that mental health relates positively to cognitive freedom, because one cannot deal enthusiastically and effectively with the many problems of life unless he operates on the assumption that he has some measure of autonomy. In order to sustain the zest associated with mental health, it is necessary to experience at least some occasional success, especially in coping with problems that are taxing. It is difficult to see how this success could be maintained without the use of cognitive skills.

Those who seek the easy option life and who have expensive appetites cannot succeed without being blessed with adequate wealth. But this combination of desire and means is not sufficient to produce mental health, because the quick satiation of the physical appetites is hardly enough to support the kind of gusto in a healthy mentality. If the claims of naive hedonism, however, were valid, the easy option life should produce the best results, including robust mental health.

Cognitive freedom cannot occur without both internal and external constraint. The internal variety is simply self-control; the other kind represents the barriers needed to define problems. Self-control is necessary to suppress impulse so that the cognitive skills can have the time to swing into action. But those skills serve no purpose if no challenge or problems exist. The ideal world of naive hedonism, with its absence of both constraints, renders cognitive freedom meaningless. But since the real world is filled with ample problems, the easy option attitude is unrealistic and is therefore irrelevant to mental health.

Dreams of utopia have intrigued people for centuries. The popular idea of utopia is a society in which all needs plus any reasonable desires are easily fulfilled. In short, it is a land of perpetual success, without strife and injustice and misery. This popular conception, however, is more idealistic than conceived by most writers on the topic from Plato to Skinner. E. H. Harbison, who studied the literature on utopia with considerable insight, identified the common premises shared by a number of writers on the subject, beginning with the works of Sir Thomas More. These premises are humanistic in tone and may be considered value assumptions of a moral nature. I will paraphrase them as follows: (a) The ideal society should be egalitarian, that is, the distribution of necessities and other goods should be equal for all. (b) All forms of individualism that tend toward the creation of inequality or exploitation should be precluded by design. (c) General happiness pretty much requires both personal integrity and innocence. (d) Quality of life is determined by the environment. Hence, the making of utopia depends considerably upon shaping the proper environment. (e) Education is essential for adequate human development. (f) Above all, human nature must be considered as essentially good, that is, we must learn to trust it and be guided by its proclivities.

Actual settlements designed to establish utopias have been based on a variety of doctrines, including both religious and secular communism. It is believed, however, that the above premises are reasonably representative of utopianism, although important exceptions exist.

One pervasive theme that undergirds utopianism is the notion that security is a necessary condition for both happiness and human welfare. Hence, utopian structures always make provisions for security. These structures tend to be rigid in order to preserve organizational integrity.

I suspect that the many failures of utopian communities spring from tensions produced by standardization, which fails to accommodate the scope of creative tendencies among the members. Unfortunately, creativity tends to produce inequality, because its very existence highlights individual differences rather than the more common elements among humans. Uniqueness is the bane of communism, which rests fundamentally on common traits. As individual differences become more and more in evidence, people tend to form social layers, grouping themselves by similarities and separating groups by gross differences. Thus, hierarchies are established, because the different social layers absorb unequal portions of power. This kind of stratification has occurred in the Soviet Union; and if the trend continues, it may doom the whole communistic structure. In other words, cognitive freedom is basically at odds with utopian philosophy and with all other doctrines that stress common features of human nature to the exclusion and suppression of personal uniqueness.

The somewhat bittersweet conclusion of these thoughts on utopia is that many people have irrepressible tendencies to express cognitive freedom, but in so doing the humanistic ideals of utopianism crumble with the emergence of a new social hierarchy. Despite all its shortcomings, democracy appears to be the only condition that succeeds in making some reasonable compromise between utopian ideals and the irresistible forces of cognitive freedom.

FOR FURTHER READING

MEDLIN, W. K., CAVE, W. M., and CARPENTER, F. *Education and Development in Central Asia: A Case Study on Social Change in Uzbekistan.* Leiden, The Netherlands: E. J. Brill Press, 1971.

Index